Bronze
Bell
Wreck

TOM BENNETT

Bronze Bell Wreck

TOM BENNETT

For Sailors' Institute

Barmouth

© TOM Bennett 2017

BRONZE BELL WRECK

12 miles North of Barmouth on the West Wales Coast, just 400 metres off a remote beach lies an Historic Shipwreck.

This is the story of how the wreck was found, why it was designated under the Protection of Wrecks Act 1973, the artefacts so far discovered and the research done to identify the ship's nationality and name.

All proceeds of this book go to the Sailors' Institute, Barmouth, a charity whose members help to keep the Ty Gwyn Museum open.

Bronze Bell Wreck   TOM BENNETT

Introduction

The "Bronze Bell" site was Designated under the Protection of Wrecks Act 1973, in the year 1979. As one of the first objects found on the site was a bronze bell, that is the name the site is known by. The wreck lies in less than 10 metres of water some 400 metres off Bennar Beach, Dyffryn Ardudwr near Talybont, North Wales. At the time of writing the name of this shipwreck is not known but her year of sinking is known. At Barmouth, is a museum which is entirely dedicated to this shipwreck and holds a collection of artefacts from the site.

My aim in writing this book was twofold. I had an ambition to keep searching all the old records until I could identify the name of the ship and her actual date of sinking. Secondly to produce a book, available at the Ty Gwyn Museum, to provide visitors with more information on the artefacts and what is currently known about the Bronze Bell Ship.

Of the known 435 shipwrecks in the area, there are very few recorded as being lost before the eighteenth century. Thus we have to start with what has been identified from the wreck site. The artefacts in the Bronze Bell Wreck Collection, the anchors, the cannon, the pewter plates, coins and seals, and of course the main cargo of marble blocks. These are all pieces of the jigsaw puzzle needed to be researched to find the name and date of sinking of this mystery ship.

CONTENTS

CONTENTS (continued)

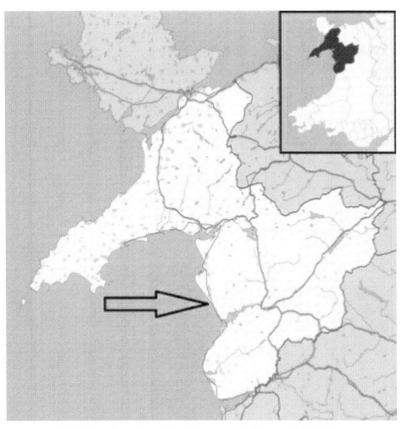

A map of Wales showing the County of Gwynedd. The arrow locates the position of the Bronze Bell wreck within Cardigan Bay. 12 miles South of the wreck site is Barmouth, that sits at the mouth of a natural estuary that extends 15 miles landwards into the mountains of North Wales. The area near Barmouth used to be in the old administrative district of Merionethshire, now Gwynedd. The Bronze Bell ship was wrecked within site of the Lord of the Manor, Vaughans, the most eminent family in Merionethshire.

Bronze Bell Wreck   TOM BENNETT

Amateur diving around the Welsh coast commenced about 1968. Over the next decade diving clubs proliferated. British Sub Aqua Club branches and Independent Clubs trained their members both to dive safely to a high standard and to enthuse them into the wonders of this new environment. It was an expensive sport and the Clubs were often run as highly efficient organizations, some specialized in various underwater disciplines. Avocational divers became interested in photography, underwater flora and fauna or shipwrecks. Others, being inspired by Jacques Cousteau and Mel Fisher searched for treasure ships. In the early 1970's as soon as magnetometers came on the scene, searches were made over hundreds of miles of Welsh coastline for such wrecks as the fictitious **Santa Cruz,** supposedly lost off the West Wales coast in 1679. Metal detecting was in its infancy and people had just started looking for coins and jewellery on beaches. Lyn Jones, living near Cardigan, a member of our newly formed Fishguard Sub Aqua Club purchased an underwater metal detector. It was a hand held one, Irish made and accordingly coloured green, specifically designed for looking for coins on wreck sites. Club members experimented with it on a few known wrecks but soon realized that it was useless as there was too much iron on UK wreck sites. This pioneer detector did not discriminate out the ferrous. A certain Geraint Jones (perhaps related to Lyn) at this time was detecting and finding coins on the beach at Talybont. He presumed a wreck was not far away. When he saw members of Glaslyn Sub Aqua Club diving from a boat 300 yards from his coin site he reported the fact to the Receiver of Wreck. Fortunately the Club had already informed the Receiver of Wreck of their wreck site. In July 1979 the Bronze Bell was found by members of the Glaslyn BSAC and three members of Harlow BSAC Branch. One was doing their first sea dive! Tony Iles, the late Mike Bower and others formed the Cae Nest Special Project Group to study the wreck. From being a non swimmer Geraint quickly learnt how to dive and was extremely enthusiastic until he learnt that no excavation permit was going to be allowed on the Bronze Bell site.

Bronze Bell Wreck   TOM BENNETT

From the date on the bell and the dating of pewter plates found, it was obvious they had found a shipwreck site of historical interest. The Cae Nest Group and the Welsh Institute of Maritime Archaeology and History at the University of Wales (Bangor) applied for site designation and a licence to survey and excavate the site. The diving magazines and the Welsh newspapers, covered the story of the Bronze Bell Wreck. One such article was written by Tony Iles entitled "Our Bronze Bell, the Magic, the Mystery and the Misery".

The misery was the fact that CADW had decided to not allow the very diving group that had surveyed the site an excavation permit. The legacy of this misery is still reflected in this book, A conference of "Underwater Archaeology in Wales", organised by Robert Kennedy at Scolton Manor in Pembrokeshire collected together interested parties.

This was about 1979 and I was invited to speak together with Sydney Wignall. It was my first meeting with Sydney Wignall, Aled Eames, Owain Roberts and members of the Cae Nest Project group. Kennedy agreed to help the group acting as conservator for the bell and the iron banded swivel gun, the first two artefacts that had been recovered. Syd, holding a pewter plate from the wreck, asked me did I know anything about them and how to date them. I confessed limited knowledge and replied that he would know far more about the subject than myself. I did however tell him that if he wanted to know about dating cannon the person to contact was Richard Larn.

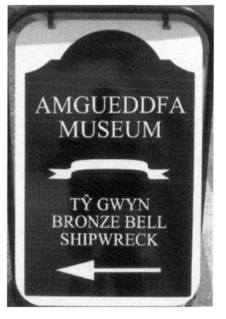

Bronze Bell Wreck   TOM BENNETT

The Government authorities, quite correctly, did not want to see an important wreck site destroyed by looting and indiscriminate excavation. This is what had happened on the **Mary,** the King's Yacht on the Skerries, off Holyhead. The Royal Yacht **Mary,** wrecked 1675, was discovered in 1971. Many important artefacts of Charles II including bronze cannon and silver candelabras were stolen from the site, some by professional divers. It was the catalyst to bring about legislation to protect such historic sites. The **Mary** was the first site in Wales to receive designation in January 1974. Ironically, the looting of the **Mary** site may have meant less interest and, less removal of artefacts from the Bronze Bell site. However the government agency by protecting the Bronze Bell Wreck, forbade the very divers who were interested in the site to carry on with an archaeological dig. The site is designated as a Historic Wreck under the Protections of Wrecks Act 1973. The protected area is a radius of 300 metres from the co-ordinate 52° 46.73'N 04° 07.53'W.
Diving or any interference including filming, survey and excavation within the protected area of a designated wreck is a criminal offence unless a license has first been obtained from the Welsh Assembly Government. CADW should be contacted in the first instance. *http://www.cadw.wales.gov.uk/.* If a licence is granted CADW will still not allow the licensee to look for or take any artefacts from the seabed at the wreck site. Not only that but they expect in return an annual report on the condition of the site, all to be done free gratis at the expense of the licensee. CADW may have protected the site but they have also suppressed enthusiastic budding archaeologists from looking at this site and any others. It is no wonder that criticism is now thrown at this organisation for little progress in Underwater Archaeology in Wales over that the last 50 years. This is the very same organization that has paid professionals to promote and encourage our Maritime Heritage.

The 1970's was a time when sports divers were keen to know more about Underwater Archaeology. The British Sub Aqua Clubs were educating and training their members into the skills required. I was part organiser of an 'Introductory Course to Underwater Archaeology' at Fishguard Further Education Centre. It was a basic course on how to map and survey a wreck site. Use of grid lines, how to research and how to conserve. A rather fruitless exercise considering the authorities did not intend to let amateurs anywhere near historic sites anyway.

Robert Kennedy at Pembrokeshire Museums was keen to help the Cae Nest Group and offered to conserve some of the artefacts already raised at the Bronze Bell Wreck site. Like many museum officials he took exception to most sports divers and thus got no respect or artefacts in return. New ship wreck sites were being found every few months and nobody apart from the divers seemed to have any interest. I felt a responsibility to record and photograph and publish something about the diving wrecks. Robert promoted himself to become a NAS (Nautical Archaeology Society) representative for Wales. In the early 1970's he once asked me for my help with my diver friends in raising the 1843 beam engine from the **Nimrod,** a paddle steamship lost off St David's. I had to tell him in no uncertain terms that it was going to stay on the seabed until he could convince me that he had the expertise and funding for its proper conservation. That may have been the catalyst for him to learn something about how to replace sea salts in iron objects so stop them falling apart. A few years later he showed me at Scolton Manor some electrolysis baths with a piece of chain from Newgale Beach that had been bubbling away for years. I asked him which end of Newgale was it found. When he told me, I could tell him the probable vessel it had come from. I regarded a piece of anchor chain from a 1917 ketch, not worth preserving, especially as he did not know of its origin. I now realize it was his test piece to understand the electrolysis process. He may have been making preparations to conserve the Bronze Bell swivel gun.

Bronze Bell Wreck   TOM BENNETT

Kennedy had a particular dislike for South Wales divers. He regarded them as underwater scrap merchants, taking everything from every wreck they find. His opinion had some foundation but he did not need to repeat it to the divers that genuinely wished to help him. His lack of understanding and respect for sports divers was reciprocated and I believe progress in Underwater Archaeology in Wales was stifled because of it. It has only come to my memory that he told me (about 1975) that divers had found four cannon in St Bride's Bay. His professionalism did not tell me the whereabouts which I respected. However it did form a big rift in our relationship as until then I used to keep him informed of all items of historical importance that were being discovered. It took me a long time to work out where and what this mystery wreck was. It should have had designation as an historic shipwreck. The sports divers who found it did not have the time to do a survey themselves or the inclination to pay for a proper survey of the site. Consequently Kennedy could not organise or fund an archaeological survey, so he kept the whole thing quiet. It appears to be a secret he has taken with him to his grave as nobody, apart from the original divers, seem to know anything about it. By not telling anyone of the wreck-site, Kennedy may have done the correct thing. The site by being unrecognised has been preserved for future generations. The illegal removal of the cannon, has been minimised. Fifty years has now elapsed since it was first reported to Kennedy. I have not dived on the wreck site and know of no recent salvage although I understand that the site was partially salvaged in the 18th Century. As the Cae Nest Group have not been allowed to salvage the Bronze Bell wreck, I should perhaps tell the Group about this historic wreck before informing CADW!

Robert Kennedy and other museum authorities may have considered that the shipwreck books I was writing only encouraged more irresponsible diving. That it may have done, but these books were the first to introduce Welsh shipwrecks to divers and the public at large.

They were the first books to have an index of Welsh wrecks in chronological order. I considered my books promoted the seeds for positive historical wreck research, at a time when few others were doing so. These Indexes were just the tip of a massive database of Welsh wreck information that had taken me many years to compile. This information, the largest database of Welsh Shipwrecks in existence, has not been passed over to the Royal Commission of Historic Monuments, for a multitude of reasons.

When any wreck is located in Wales, reference is first made to the Hydrographic Department records to see what has been recorded by them when making the Admiralty Charts and information received from the Receiver of Wreck. If nothing seen, then databases are scanned to see if Larn and Larn Shipwreck Index no.5 or original indexes in my books and those of Carl Smith and Chris Holden, (see References at end of book) can shed any light on the wreck. These indexes are not complete but they do provide an excellent starting point. Although an advocate of the Protection of Wrecks Act 1973, I have always been critical of how CADW has made its own interpretation and implementation of the legislation throughout Wales.

A small part of a Viking sword was found off Pembrokeshire in 1991 by sports divers from Milton Keynes Sub Aqua Club. The 900 year old object is exquisite, a superb example of Viking art and their skill as craftsmen.

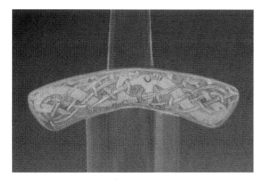

**Viking sword hilt from the Smalls Wreck site.
Photo © Mark Rednap, National Museum of Wales.**

It is regarded as one of the National Treasures of Wales.

Bronze Bell Wreck   TOM BENNETT

WASAC (Welsh Association of Sub Aqua Clubs) the official voice for both British Sub Aqua Clubs and Independent Clubs, gave their specialist advice on the Smalls Historic Wreck before its designation.. None of the advice was heeded. The Secretary of State for Wales via CADW and the National Museum of Wales designated the site. I am sure the definition of a wreck does not include one third of one small object. Nevertheless, designated as a Historic Wreck site it was with no appreciation of the adverse consequences and not being able to enforce the legislation. Legally it meant The Smalls group of islands was out of bounds to divers, one of the best diving sites in Europe. Being a spokesman for WASAC and being in a position to help CADW, my enthusiasm and thousands of other divers was decidedly thwarted.

Mark Redknap, National Museum Director has always been cooperative with metal detectorists and sports divers. He organized a video and survey of the Small's Site a few years later. I have always maintained that if there was no designation, the sports divers would themselves be in a position to tell the authorities if there was a Viking wreck there or not. Should there be a wreck, the Museum would have received many more artefacts if they had taken advice from WASAC and not gone ahead with any designation.

Syd Wignall, (1922-2012) may have had his faults when compared to the disciplines involved and required in Underwater Archaeology today; but he was a pioneer, a character with a passion to inspire others. He was frustrated that CADW was not allowing the Cae Nest Group to excavate and find more interesting artefacts. These factors may be fading slowly into the past, but they are part of the story of struggle and misery that must be told of the Bronze Bell Wreck and the Ty Gwyn Museum.

In 2016, there were forums and comments about how it was generally regarded that Maritime Heritage and Underwater Archaeology in Wales over the last two decades has not progressed. At last the historic environment service of the Welsh Government is interested through their Coflein mapping of wreck sites around the coast of Wales. Over the last eleven years their Maritime Officers have been mapping and adding references to known wrecks around the coast.

Bronze Bell Wreck   TOM BENNETT

The text and references are excellent but they are not proof read before being released onto the Coflein map seen by the public. Topographical errors and their positioning on the Coflein map is so hopeless that it makes a mockery of the whole system.

The main aim is to produce a comprehensive and accurate Shipwreck Database, to record what is existing and to aid further research. I am so disappointed and frustrated that this is not happening. Coflein have tried hard to secure a proper database of shipwrecks but in many cases are relying on Larn's latitude and longitude, and think that this is a true position of the named wreck. It may be a known wreck but the position is certainly not known on 90% of the entries. Even the identified diving wreck sites, well documented by myself and many others in the sports diving fraternity, have not yet been entered on the Coflein Map. These should have been the first wrecks to be recorded, at least ten years ago. Should the Welsh Government find the inclination to contract me as a Maritime Officer, I would be more than happy to correct, improve and help them produce a Welsh Database of Wrecks that would be beyond criticism. After all, this is something I have been attempting to do myself for the last forty years, with no payment whatsoever. Governments have still not understood how to treat divers or treasure seekers in a fair way. Look at the recent court case of Spain v Odyssey Marine. Treasure from a Spanish Wreck in international waters was determined to belong to the Spanish Government and had to be returned to Spain with no salvage compensation. It is a travesty of justice not understood by the authorities. All Spanish artefacts in the future are not likely to be declared. It immediately has stopped researchers bothering to look for Spanish Treasure Ships. Treasure hunters, so despised, yet essential for the establishments will seek other treasures. Spanish treasures will be discovered but Spain will not be informed. Artefacts and silver will be recovered but not declared. Precious items will be sold over the Internet and we will have lost a valuable resource. Museums, Spanish Heritage, as well as our greater knowledge of 15th to 18th Century sea trading and ship construction, will be the losers.

Bronze Bell Wreck   TOM BENNETT

What if Denmark, Norway or Ireland were to say that the Sword hilt found on The Smalls belongs to them, because it came off a Viking boat belonging to that country? Do we say OK, you can have it back now to put in one of your museums? I don't think so. However you can just imagine where such reasoning can lead us.

If a Spanish treasure ship sinks as a result of it being overpowered by an English Man O' War, I would maintain it is justifiably English booty and not Spanish anyway.

Enough of my griping, I had better return to the Bronze Bell Wreck. So named because the bell was one of the first iconic artefacts to be recovered. When it was designated an Historic Shipwreck, the site was already being referred to by that name as the true name of the ship was not known. I commenced my research into identifying the wreck site before reading the Wessex Archaeology Report of 2006 which suggested the 1709 date of sinking. My research started assuming the ship to be a French one wrecked 1690 -1703. This failed to come up with anything but I did learn a lot about the political events of the day. The English Navy were capturing French vessels and taking them as a prize and renaming them.

Calendar of State Papers can now be viewed online. Although the author has failed to find any reference to the Bronze Bell wreck in those documents. These papers give the full political flavour of ship taxes, where troops were being shipped and the general prejudice shown towards Southern Ireland and Catholic France. Immigration policies were being established with unwanted Catholics from the Palatines (Rhine area of Germany) being sent home if they happened to arrive unexpectedly from a shipwreck on the shores of UK. Even Wales had a strong anti-Catholic hatred as two priests were grisly hung drawn and quartered on the streets of Cardiff at the time for no apparent reason other than their Faith.

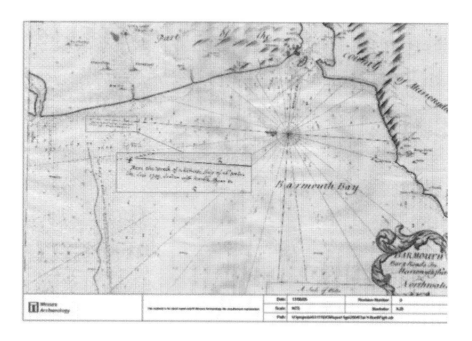

CADW commissioned Wessex Archaeology to study, survey and write up an Underwater Archaeology Report of the site. This can be seen online. A friend of Mike Bowyer was looking through early charts at The Hydrographic Office in Taunton, when he came across this early chart, a copy is now held at Gwynedd Archives. It was a lucky find. A handwritten statement is seen on the chart in the same position as the Bronze Bell Wreck site.

X *Here the Wreck of a Genoese Ship, of ab't 700 tun Lies. Lost 1709. Laden with Marble, Paper etc.*

The position exactly matches the location of the Bronze Bell site. This not only gives us the year the shipwreck occurred but also the size of the ship. Accuracy and diligence to detail is one of the requirements of a Cartographer and all the information and the location can be assumed to be correct.

Bronze Bell Wreck   TOM BENNETT

This first chart showing the Barmouth area is one made by Lewis Morris and William Morris, cartographers. It was not available to the Captain of the Bronze Bell ship as the chart was made and printed in 1748.

Realizing thousands of documents can be seen now online I had a desire to research all aspects of the Bronze Bell Wreck in the hope that I would come across the specific date within 1709 and the actual name of the ship. Richard and Bridget Larn's Shipwreck Index of the British Isles published in 2000, is often used as the most convenient reference source for shipwrecks. Sources used in this Index include Lloyds List, Board of Trade Wreck Registers, other books and wreck lists. Unfortunately, from these records neither myself or Richard Larn found any mention of a shipwreck happening in 1709 in Merionethshire.

The date, predates newspapers in Wales by about a century. Some news was being printed in London in 1709, notably the London Gazette, which can now be viewed online. The chart description with the cross was probably written about forty years after the event. The way it is written suggests that the wreck was still lying there. If the one making the note on the chart knew the name of the ship, he would have put the name of the ship onto the chart entry. By putting the estimated tonnage, he is identifying the vessel as he did not have any name of the wreck.

Two Wrecks at the wreck site ?
As two coins have been found that are centuries earlier than wreck site date, there was the presumption that the site had two wrecks, one lying on top of the other. A Government based educational website http://education.gtj.org.uk/en/item10/25499"Gathering the Jewels" is to inspire and enthuse people into understanding British history and culture through Museum collections. This website is suggesting two wrecks on the site, a theory that develops more credibility as this book progresses.

In the summer of 1978, members of a local sub-aqua team discovered the wreck of a heavily-armed galleon off the shore of Dyffryn Ardudwy (between Barmouth and Harlech, Merionethshire). It is thought that the ship foundered there in 1709, followed by a second ship, years later, which lay on top of the first wreck. Among the many finds were a fine bronze bell which bears the inscription 'Laudate Dominus Omnes Gente' (All people praise the Lord), and the date 1671.[1677] One of the ships was also carrying a large cargo of precious Carrara marble from Genoa, Italy. (Reference Gathering the Jewels")*

The two wrecks theory is due to several anomalies;

1) Undated coins typical of 14th and 15th Century found on site. *(Ref. Geraint Jones).*

2) The matching array of armed, wrought iron swivel guns which date back to to pieces used by the French in the Burgundian Wars, in the 15th Century.

3)Pre Disturbance Survey 1982, which shows a differing outline for the swivels to the later, larger 1709 wreck *(Ref. Iles. T. Cymru A'r Mor, 2005, Issue No. 26).*

4) Shipwrecks tend to happen in the same place, especially at nearby Sarn Badrig. At many wreck sites there are wrecks that lie on top of other ones.

When I commenced this review, I was convinced that there was only one ship on this wreck site and all artefacts recovered were from the same ship. However Tony Iles, reminded me, mentioning that the array of early swivel guns did not seem to match the armaments of the Bronze Bell wreck. If the swivel guns are indeed 200 years older than the "marble wreck" then this does put doubt into my mind. However, some swivel guns were likely on the Bronze Bell Ship, but not from the 15th Century. They are often on the poop and upper decks thus they may scatter in a different manner when the hull collapses. Only six swivel guns have been seen, all appearing much older than the Bronze Bell wreck. Some swivel guns were found under the larger iron cannon, implying they were already on the seabed when the Bonze Bell Ship sank.

The two wreck theory would be confirmed if a 15th Century ship's bell Were to be discovered on the site.

Bronze Bell Wreck   TOM BENNETT

If we continue the theory that there was another wreck at the site, then all the smallest cannon and swivel guns could be from this earlier wreck. I maintain that if the Bronze Bell ship was grounded for two weeks, and her mast and rigging systematically removed, then all her swivel guns would also have been salvaged.

We thus have to calculate, where high and low water was on the ship when she was being salvaged or stuck on the reef. I am assuming that it was a vessel with three decks. The cannon would be on the second deck level. If this was permanently underwater, it would make removal of these armaments much more difficult. This may be why they remained inside the hull until it broke apart. Just like the mast and rigging the smaller deck armaments could easily be salvaged. If they did not find their way to Harlech Castle they would have been taken with the masts to Dublin and on to a Naval dockyard, like Chatham, London.

The depth of water around the wreck site is about 6 to 7.5 metres depth at Low Water Neap tides. The range of tide, even if not on Springs can be 4.5 metres. Draught of vessel estimated 5 metres. Thus at any low water, especially with a swell of one metre a large vessel can hit a reef sticking up only one metre above the seabed.

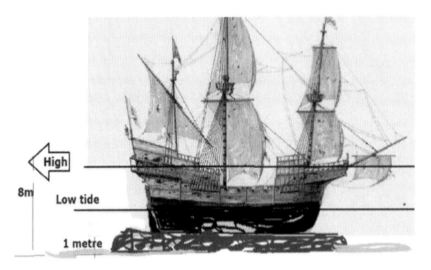

My theory of the wrecking process, is that the Bronze Bell Ship got taken into that part of Cardigan Bay by stress of weather. By the time the captain realized he was in the wrong place he was trying to sail out of trouble. The wind had died down and the ship was being sailed cautiously around Sarn Badrig from the south but unluckily hit an unknown reef when in very shallow water. My theory further maintains that the ship grounded and stuck on the reef in an upright fashion, allowing those on board time to abandon without loss of life. Also that the ship lay upright half submerged for two weeks while partial salvage took place.

The largest known tidal range in Barmouth is 5.19 m (17 feet) Draught of vessel (waterline to keel) estimated 4.87 metres or 16 feet Height of reef above seabed of sand; 1 metre (3 feet). Some of the biggest tides in each year are the Equinoctials in March when the depth of water at Low Water may only be 0.3 metres above Chart Datum. I think the vessel stranded one month before the biggest Spring Tides. Stranding when unable to get off is often associated with not Low tide but about 2 hours before Low Tide . We know there were strong Westerly winds on 3rd February which could make two meter swells at Bennar Beach. The ship running onto a reef with a heavy cargo can be slammed on to rocks with any swell quickly piercing the wooden hull. The captain may have thought he was sailing in 25 feet of water, even with a swell was not a problem. He has 10 feet of water under his keel. An unidentified reef sticking 3 feet above the seabed is giving him only 7 feet of clearance. At the bottom of a large swell the ship can easily hit. Morris's chart shows depth of water at the wrecks site about one fathom (6 feet) at chart datum. A big swell can also lift the ship off the reef but if unlucky will only slam it down again a bit further along the same reef. Three such poundings and the ship would be sinking on top of the reef. The ship may sink down only 4 or 7 feet lower than her waterline ie to deck level. As the tide is still dropping, those on board can still walk the decks and collect some of their possessions. The ship stays upright. However as the tide rises the water level is another 10 feet higher than the deck amidships and just covers the higher poop deck on the stern castle.

Bronze Bell Wreck   TOM BENNETT

If this happened some days before a Spring Tide, the Low Water height gets lower each day. As the Low Water gets lower it means they can reach cargo in the lower parts of the hold.

A variety of disciplines, knowledge and research skills are needed to investigate the identity of the Bronze Bell wreck and the specific date of her sinking.
1. A close look is needed on what was happening politically throughout Europe at the time.
2. A study of Church and Manorial Records.
3 A study of predominant gales or unusual weather
4 A thorough examination of shipwreck lists already published.
5 An examination of the marble cargo
6 An examination of the cannon and their number found at the site.
7 A supposition of where a paper and marble cargo were going.
8. Identity and in numeration of all the coins found
9 A look at the seals and artefacts recovered.
10 Appreciation of why shipwrecks occur at Sarn Badrig.
11 A study of artefacts and timbers at Cors y Gedol Hall
12 Investigation of Juan Benedictus and other names.
13 A study of the size, dimensions and shape of the three anchors.
14 A study of the bell, its foundry and significance

This book investigates these aspects but not in any particular order. There is an acceptance that the marble has been identified correctly and the artefacts at the Ty Gwyn Museum relate to this shipwreck site. The entry on the chart mentions marble, paper etc. I want to start with investigating what these other goods may have been. Marble was invariably loaded at Leghorn, now named Livorno, a port ninety miles south of Genoa, Italy. Wines, olive oils, soaps, ladies' hats, also muslins and silks are the goods likely covered by the "etc". This list is taken from an incoming Leghorn cargo some forty years later. Leghorn was known for its hats. There is a Leghorn Hat with a large brim and a Leghorn Bonnet lined with muslin and lace. All evidence of these items would be lost to the sea if they were on the ship in the first place.

Paper cargo

The Republic of Genoa, the coastal region at the North end of Italy, was at the forefront of printing and of paper production in the year 1709. The best writing paper came from France, the best printing paper from Holland and Genoa. Both the cargo of paper and marble was likely loaded in the ports of Genoa or Leghorn both within the Republic of Genoa. The fact that paper is mentioned as the second most important cargo gives additional credence the vessel had loaded in the Republic of Genoa. In London on 9th February in the London Gazette is advertised a new Folio Bible that had just been printed and was available at Her Majesties Bookshop in Black Friars and the Bible bookshop in Ave Mary Lane, it was said to be printed on good paper. In 1711 there was paper known as 'Genoa Paper', and 'Genoa Royal', a high quality creamy white paper. It was sold by the ream for three shillings and three pence, a lot of money in those days. This year, 1709, the British Government considered imposing an Import Tax on the importation of cards, and then later paper, so as to preserve the paper industry in Britain. The Lewis Morris chart entry mentions that the ship carried both paper and marble as a cargo. This snippet of information may help us understand where the marble was destined for. Paper, in any year, would have been a useful cargo going to London, Paris or Amsterdam. Albeit any big European city would want paper, especially if the price was right. Richard Steele produced 271 issues of 'The Tatler' from 12 April 1709. This was the Savoy printers in London. This would require a large amount of paper, but I have seen no reference to paper being imported from Genoa for this purpose. The Import Tax on paper implies that paper imports into London would fall after the date of 1712. Paper made in Genoa was of the highest quality. There had already been generations of paper makers who would keep the secrets of their manufacture very close to their chests, as it was an important and growing export for Genoa.

We are told that paper from the wreck washed up on the shore. As I have never come across any description of the wrecking process, I have my doubts as to the authenticity of this fact. Paper packed tightly in boxes is not likely to float ashore, although I can quite imagine them to be salvaged from the wreck and dumped on the beach. I presume paper would be boxed flat in crates that could be carried by two men. If paper did indeed wash ashore at the time of the wrecking, they were probably the upper cargo that was thrown over to lighten the ship. I have found no reference as to what became of the paper cargo. Whoever added the wreck information onto the chart was confident that the vessel was Genoese. A "Genoese Ship" implies more that it belonged to that Port and owned by a Genoese company than meaning it had come from that port. The ship may have assumed to be a Genoese ship because it had a cargo of Italian marble and paper from that port on board. What is somewhat odd is that nobody has mentioned the name of the vessel. If William Morris knew her name he would have added that to the chart. The mention of the correct cargo on the chart gives further clues. It was known to Morris, some forty years later, that the cargo was marble and paper. It would have been a big event for that area and he would have known much more about the wreck, if there was a big loss of life and if marble and paper was salvaged. He must have acquired this knowledge from people living locally. Such people may themselves have been survivors of the wreck who knew the cargo. Local people may have seen stone blocks or paper being salvaged from the wreck, or even helped in their salvage. An Italian, a foreigner to the area, was buried in the local churchyard some 21 years later in 1730. He may have been illiterate but even if a crew member he surely could have given a ship's name if it were known to him.

It is documented that Cors y Gedol had a very extensive library. Although many books existed there before 1709 it is not beyond reason that more books may have been acquired by exchange for salvaged paper. All the London printers published books to supplement their business's.

Marble Blocks

The marble blocks at the site provide a major clue as to the identity of the ship. The main cargo lies amidships and consists of approximately 66 tonnes of marble, comprising 42 blocks ranging in size from 800 cm (31 inch) cubes to blocks measuring 2.8m x 1m x 0.8 m (9ft x 3ft x 2.5ft). 3600 lbs weight or 1.6 tons (1632 kg). With typical blocks being 1.55 x 0.75 x 0.65 m. Two blocks were recently recovered under licence, of which one has been carved by the local artist, the late Frank Cocksey. It is named 'The Last Haul', a carving depicting three generations of fishermen hauling in their nets for the last time.

The "Last Haul" by local sculptor Frank Cocksey, made from Carrara marble recovered under licence from the wreck site.

It is to be seen on the seafront at Barmouth.
Photograph courtesy of www.tywynholidays.co.uk

Bronze Bell Wreck   TOM BENNETT

Although I was aware that others had associated the Bronze Bell Ship cargo as intended for St Paul's, I had to look at other destinations. Searching through all the statues of Europe and the eminent buildings being constructed in Dublin, Edinburgh, Amsterdam and Hamburg, I could find little information. I then commenced looking at Paris. The Royal Chapel at Versailles which was built with a good deal of Carrara marble was completed in 1710. All marble from Carrara would be loaded at the port of Leghorn (Livorno) and sailed out of the Mediterranean through the Straits of Gibraltar and northwards across the Bay of Biscay and then east into the English Channel. Ships would enter the River Seine near Le Havre and then up the tortuous river to Paris. However in February and March 1709, northern France was in the grip of one of the biggest 'Frosts' ever recorded. Temperatures were more akin to the arctic and the Seine River was totally iced over making passage impossible for ships. "Aha," I thought, a ship carrying marble was diverted to Dublin because she could not get up the frozen Seine in March 1709. Built by Louise XIV, The Royal Chapel it is regarded as one of the most exquisite of all religious buildings. He used the Chapel for five years before his death. The French wars during the nine years previous to 1709 had slowed up the building of this most magnificent chapel. The Italians could do trade directly with the Dutch during this time and we know Carrara marble shipments were going to Amsterdam during this period. In 1708 two marble ships were taken as a prize when off the French coast. One theory of how a French boat could be carrying a cargo of Italian marble is that it was transshipped from a captured Dutch vessel onto a French vessel in Dunkirk and ended up in Cardigan Bay. Other nations, eg Albania were allowed to trade with both Italy and France and have immunity from the French corsairs. A Ragusan (definition later) vessel could trade with Leghorn and with any other European country. Such a vessel could trade around the coast of France without fear of being taken as a French prize in the years 1706 to 1709. It was not unknown for merchant ships to carry a Rasugan flag on board with which to fool or ward off a French corsair attack.

This is a painting of Leghorn (Livorno) in the year 1700. A large Dutch merchant ship has just arrived and is flying a yellow Q flag to say her crew are free of Smallpox and the Plague and she requires Health Clearance. The ship is light (riding high in the water) and wants to pick up a marble cargo. A cannon is being fired from her port side, perhaps a sign of impatience. Knowing that the French King could obtain marble via the Dutch somewhat dispels my previous notion that the Bronze Bell Ship was heading for Versailles. My initial interest in Versailles was that others had suggested from the artefacts recovered that the vessel may be of French origin. Now I think otherwise.

Bronze Bell Wreck   TOM BENNETT

We do not know if the marble block mound on the seabed is the entire cargo of the ship when she sank or if there was salvage in the months or years immediately after the wrecking. Although I have no proof as yet, I would have thought that a ship of 700 tons would have carried five times as many blocks. Also, that salvage of some of these would have taken place in 1709 and 1710.

Mike Bower, Tony Iles and the BBC did research into where the blocks came from and the likely intended destination. One would think that if blocks had been salvaged then a salvage team would have recovered the entire cargo. Lifting a one ton rectangular block from the seabed is awkward even in relatively shallow water. The depth is not a problem but a diver would need to put ropes around the blocks to do a tidal lift using the buoyancy of a larger boat. It is time consuming and would require salvage boats, divers, lifting block and tackle and about 20 men. However marble blocks of this quality have always been valuable and one has to reason that if some blocks were salvaged why did the team leave so much of this cargo still on the seabed. The author is of the opinion that up to forty blocks were salvaged soon after the grounding. While writing this text, the thought occurred to me that the ship may not have broken up the day it grounded but may have remained with its masts up for some days, or even weeks, after the event. This would have enabled blocks to be lifted out of the hold before the ship broke up. This is why we see three anchors still remaining on the wreck site. If any underwater salvage had been carried out the first items recovered would have been the anchors. An individual anchor would have had a value greater than one block and be easier to retrieve. I surmise that if the wreck had happened in Cornwall or on the South Coast of England where salvage divers were more available, the entire marble consignment would have been recovered. Albeit, it would be far cheaper recovering white marble blocks from an 8 metre depth wreck site in Cardigan Bay than importing the same again from Genoa. I surmise that this was the very last Carrara marble cargo ordered for St Paul's.

The marble has been identified as originating from Carrara in Italy. It is of the highest grade white marble in the World and in the trade referred to as Statue Marble. It is white, pure and lacks fault lines. Used by the Greeks it has been the preferred material for sculptors, from Michelangelo to Henry Moore. The Tuscany quarries no longer have this marble as it has all been worked out. The blocks found on the site are already cut into standard sizes and must have been destined for some eminent or expensive building. Many large buildings and palaces were being constructed at that time throughout Europe, from Liverpool to Amsterdam. Sir Christopher Wren was the King's architect in the rebuilding of St Paul's. The original cathedral was burnt down in the Great Fire of London in 1666. In 1674 a new church was commenced, but it was decided that the cost should be borne out of a Coal Duty Tax. In that time there had been immense political and religious changes. No longer was Catholicism in vogue and the populace did not want a building venerating Catholic interests but a religious building of a more Puritanical nature. Wren favoured grand designs and wanted a church with a large dome that would dominate the London skyline. St Paul's was built over thirty years but its interior was never finished off in the manner that Wren wanted. The massive dome roof, second only in size to St Peter's in Rome, was completed around 1708. In 1709 the builders were making final arrangements to the floors, choirs and altar area. The original design of the altar was to raise it up from the floor to sit on a platform of white Carrara marble. This work was scheduled to be done in 1703/4, but was never started. It is suggested that as the final flooring and detail was being done in 1709, this altar platform was ordered by Wren to make the Altar area complete. We know this altar platform of blocks never arrived at St Paul's.

By 1709 considerable amounts of marble had already been sent from Leghorn to supply materials to build St Paul's. It is unfortunate that all the Port Books relating to these outgoing shipments were burnt. In 1887, as there were too many documents to retain, the Port authorities sold them off as fuel for domestic fires!

Bronze Bell Wreck   TOM BENNETT

When merchant ships are heavily armed, they may be carrying up to half the cannons (guns) of a similar tonnage Naval vessel. This not only means they are slower but have less cargo space, both factors make them more prone to capture from specialised pirate and corsair vessels. During the years 1704 to 1709 ships carrying goods from Italy to Northern Europe were susceptible to piracy in three distinct areas. One was near the Straits of Gibraltar where Algerian pirates in swift light galleys could board and capture the ship. The second was a pack of hunting French corsairs, perhaps three or four well armed ships in the northern Bay of Biscay and the area up to the Channel Islands. The third area was in the English Channel itself. The French corsairs would capture the British and Dutch merchant ships and take them into Dunkirk as a prize. According to the size of the vessel and an estimation of the cargo value, a considerable ransom had to be paid to the French including food and keep of the crew, before the ship could continue. For three years the French maintained a squadron at Rochefort with the sole intention of capturing or causing an embargo on English trade. To reduce the risk of capture, any ship sailing north to Britain from the Straits of Gibraltar would stay at least 50 miles off the French coast.

Photograph of the Aisle flooring in St Paul's. The black marble is a very black Belgian marble and the white the Italian Carrara. Some of the last flooring to be laid in 1708 and 1709 used black Kilkenny marble that was shipped from Dublin, Ireland.

Bronze Bell Wreck   TOM BENNETT

In 1707, there is a reference to Black Marble from Dublin, Ireland going to St Paul's. The Privy Council issued a licence to a London merchant to go to Le Havre to fetch some black Irish marble. A French privateer had captured the British ship **Unity** of London which was transporting black Irish marble from Dublin to St Paul's. The captured marble cargo was taken to Le Havre and a licence to go to buy it back from France was being issued to Francis Collins. As the two countries were at war he needed this licence otherwise trading would have been tantamount to treason. This licence was granted in December 1707. It is assumed that Collins ship was sent to Le Havre to pick up this marble, probably early in 1708 and that this Irish black marble successfully ended up in St Paul's Cathedral. This black marble, presumably from the 'Marble City' of Kilkenny, was likely used in the flooring or the steps at the west door. The main aisle flooring made of Belgian black and Italian white marble may have already been laid at this time but I believe there was flooring near to the choirs that needed finishing in 1709. The tiles are in a black and white diamond pattern and it would be interesting to know if the square size of each tile corresponds to 31 inches, the size of the cube blocks lying at the wreck site. A cube is not the usual size for a building block and the blocks found at the wreck site may have been intended to be cut into tiles for the flooring at St Paul's. The square size of the floor tiles is likely the same size block specified by Wren to construct the Altar platform. If the cube block size is the same as the floor tile, this would further add credence that the Bronze Bell Ship did have a cargo destined for St Paul's. Knowing that flooring marble was transported from Dublin in 1708, further endorses the fact that our Bronze Bell Ship may have been going to Dublin and not to London. It is far easier to sail directly to Dublin than to run the gauntlet with the French corsairs in the English Channel Syd Wignall was of the opinion the ship may have been destined for Dublin and these facts support this idea.

What we do know is that from State Papers of the Privy Council record the fact that 300 pounds was sent to William Chetwynd, resident of Genoa, to cover a bill of "extraordinaries" that he had arranged there during the period 12 January to 12th December 1708. We cannot be sure that this included marble and paper or his expenses for arranging these shipments but this is the person who would be their man in Genoa.

September 5th 1709   Same for 300*l.* to William Chetwynd, Resident with the Republic of Genoa; for a bill of extraordinaries 1708 Jan. 12 to Dec. 12 in that service.

Money for the building of St Paul's came out of a Coal Tax but payments for materials had to be approved by the Privy Council and paid via the Treasurer Lord Godolphin. (1645-1712)
The British State Papers give us names of who was involved when cargoes were being sought in Leghorn. These were important people based in Genoa, the commercial capital of the Republic. In 1709 there was a John Chetwynd (not William) her Majesty's Envoy to the Duke of Savoy, who was paid 15,000 pounds as part payment of the 45,000 pounds for troops or their provisions that he had arranged at Genoa and Turin for the uses of her Majesty's Forces in Catalonia.
William Blathwayt (Blathwaite) was an important civil servant working for the Treasury and the Admiralty, in 1697 to 1703 he organized consignments of white marble from Genoa. He was conversant in Italian and in December 1696 he had problems with the Genoese Bank of St George, over a consignment of blocks of marble and some wine he was exporting. He was clerk to the Privy Council, a civil servant working at Scotland Yard. In 1709 he ordered six tons of white marble from Genoa for somebody's tomb. This was destined for London but no more information is seen on this consignment. (Source William Blathwayt's papers). The Bronze bell cargo was at least ten times this amount, and would have been ordered at least 12 months before so this order is a different consignment to the Bronze Bell Marble. However it does show us that marble from Leghorn was still being ordered and who was in involved.

Bronze Bell Wreck   TOM BENNETT

I have no reference for it, but around 1708-9, Lord Godolphin wrote to Wren, to my very loving friend Sir Christopher Wren, Surveyor General about four ships carrying marble from Leghorn, which were subjected to quarantine. One assumes they had arrived in London.
The King of Denmark visited Leghorn in the year 1709. Perhaps he had commissioned a Genoese ship from Leghorn to take marble to Denmark during that year. Leghorn seemed to be the favoured port of export for the Carrara mines. The blocks found seem to be of two main sizes, one nearly nine foot long and the other blocks of a rectangular shape. The nine foot blocks could be intended to be sculptured into a statue at the intended destination. BBC researchers have suggested that in ledgers of St Paul's there are notes that some marble was to come via Wales and that it did not arrive. I have looked through much of the history of the building of St Paul's and have failed to find this reference, but have not seen the ledgers. It was Wren's original intention of raising the altar a few feet higher than the floor in white marble, which was not completed by the official opening date in 1711. Around 1710, Wren, had been accused of filtering off money and was directed to other building works. The reference (not seen by the author) that blocks for St Paul's were coming via Wales still does not mean the blocks were originally intended for London or St Paul's. If and when the Privy Council heard of the Bronze Bell shipwreck (in 1709) they could have suggested salvaging the blocks for the other buildings being constructed such as Blenheim Palace.
There were other buildings in Hamburg, Amsterdam and Liverpool that could have been the destination for such fine marble. St Paul's was being built and other colours of Italian marble had already been laid on its floors. Carrara marble was not, of course, the only form of white marble available. Commissioners bought marble throughout Europe, mainly coloured marbles from Northern Europe *(Wren Society, XV)*

Marble was bought regularly from 1684 to 1709 (Wren Society, XX pp. xxv— xxviii). In 1694, the site building office requested Admiral Lord Edward Russell, commander-in-chief, to arrange for collection of marble building blocks from Leghorn or Genoa. *(Wren Society, XV, p. Wren Society XVIII p.174 society, XVIII, p. 174).* Although Admiral Russell arranged it the consignment would have come on a large merchant vessel. It is assumed that these consignments duly arrived and were incorporated into the structure of St Paul's prior to 1709. What we need to find is a direct reference to a ship leaving Leghorn early in 1709 destined for Dublin or London with marble and paper. Although I have searched diligently, I have failed to find this. What is recorded is mention of statue marble blocks being in London in April 1709. The State Papers are instructing the Treasurer Godolphin to contact Christopher Wren about moving some marble.

"Same by same to Sir Christopher Wren, Surveyor General of Works, to deliver over to the Surveyor of the Works at Woodstock for the use of the Duke of Marlborough's house that is building there eight blocks of white marble at present in the Store Yard [of the Office of Works] in Scotland Yard. And further to deliver three other like blocks for the use of the cathedral church of St. Paul's, being meant by her Majesty to be employed in making her statue and pedestal at Paul's ("her statue with other ornaments to be erected and set up there")". Appending: schedule of the said eleven blocks of marble setting out their length, breadth and thickness. Ibid., p. 342. The reference for this is

'Warrant Books: April 1709, 16-30', in Calendar of Treasury Books, Volume 23, 1709, ed. William A Shaw (London, 1949), pp. 143-153. British History Online http://www.british-history.ac.uk/cal-treasury-books/vol23/pp143-153 [accessed 13 October 2017].

The above is the entry in the Calendar of Treasury Books, the originals would have more. There is no mention above as to where these marble blocks may have originated. As there is a schedule attached giving dimensions of the said blocks these may also enlighten us as to where they came from. The original document needs to be studied and the dimensions compared with those on the wreck site.

The date coincides with Bronze Bell Marble being salvaged from the site in February or March 1709. However, if these eleven blocks at Scotland Yard had come from the Bronze Bell site one has to conjecture why more blocks were not taken from the site. It could be that these were taken out of the stranded ship using her own masts as derricks to lift the 1.6 ton blocks, before the ship broke apart. The Store Yard at Scotland Yard is where goods from wrecks or prizes were stored. The Duke of Marlborough in private correspondence wrote to his wife the Duchess of Marlborough about marble at the Tower (Tower of London) being intended for a fountain at their residence being built in 1709. This was Blenheim House, now called Blenheim Palace, the same destination as the eight blocks from Scotland Yard. This reference may mean that marble blocks were unloaded at the Tower and then stored at Scotland Yard or it may refer to a different stock of marble stored at the Tower. I surmise they are the same blocks first unloaded from a ship at the Tower and then transported to Scotland Yard. By having a schedule of block dimensions attached to the letter to Christopher Wren could imply that there were lots of blocks lying at Scotland Yard and that only the eleven with the correct dimensions were to be moved. During 1707 there was still at Scotland Yard marble from a French fly boat that had been taken as a prize at Topsham, Devon in 1689 with a considerable amount of marble, some known to go to Earl of Pembroke for Blenheim Palace. *Mariners Mirror Vol 68 p 309.* It is possible, but I think unlikely, that there were still marble blocks in store at Scotland Yard in March 1709 from this earlier cargo.

The only other reference seen is again from Duke of Marlborough informing his wife that one block is to be made into a statue in the Buffet Room at Blenheim House. The marble remaining on the wreck site are of a variety of rectangular shapes and sizes. The same block sizes may have arrived in London. Amongst national documents still surviving should be references to ship landings of marble at The Tower and what was stored at Scotland Yard at any one time.

The fact that marble for an altar platform never arrived and that the platform was never built at St Paul's may be part of The Bronze Bell story. There is a distinct lack of information concerning this wreck throughout 1709. This fact, in itself, has significance and we may deduce other factors relating to the incident. First that there was not a great loss of life. Secondly that it was not wrecked on one specific date but broke up weeks after the grounding. That the ship and cargo were known to the Admiralty and the Privy Council. That as many marble blocks as could easily be salvaged were retrieved. The Lord of the Manor was Vaughan of Cors y Gedol. His mansion overlooked the wreck and he acted on behalf of the Crown. He not only declared what was being salvaged but organised recovery of some of the cargo and possessions. Had Vaughan not been involved the Port Comptroller at Caernarfon or Chester would have sent his Kings/Customs men to control salvage and then it should be documented in the Admiralty records. If blocks were salvaged then they would have been taken to Dublin. They were then under the management of the shipping agents that were accustomed to sending the Irish marble to London and St Paul's. These being the same agents that the cargo was assigned to anyway. The surviving crew and soldiers could also have taken the same route to catch an outward going vessel back to Leghorn or Genoa. This would explain why no money to repatriate the crew appears in the State Papers of the day, the Privy Council already knew of the Bronze Bell wreck and arrangements for getting the crew home was already being sorted.

My original estimation of the grounding date was 7th -14th February 1709. The date the wreck collapsed around 26th February, give or take about seven days. Time needed to get the marble to Dublin from Barmouth, two days. Unshipping and loading onto a ship to London three days to one week. Dublin to London, one week. Unloading of marble at Tower of London, two days. Moving to Scotland Yard, three days. Therefor by the end of March 1709 the marble could have been in London.

Bronze Bell Wreck   TOM BENNETT

A few anecdotal facts support the theory that the Bronze Bell Ship was carrying marble and paper intended for St Paul's. The year 1709 coincides with the year that the builders were wanting such marble blocks to make the altar platform of St Paul's and also to finish off the flooring. The blocks themselves are of various cube and rectangular sizes, which may have specifically been carved before shipment to make the altar feature. Hence only 65 tons of marble when the ship was capable of carrying six times that tonnage. The majority of the blocks look like building blocks for a platform, rather than blocks to make sculptures. Some of the blocks were nine foot long, suitable for carving a statue. Blocks being transported at sea are better being rectangular shaped as they can be packed tighter and less liable to move or slip when under boisterous conditions. The whole of Europe was desperately short of paper and there were at least four major printers in London that were printing Bibles and other popular books on expeditions and anatomy. In the grounds of St Paul's was 'Phoenix' one of the principle printers in London. They were in need of printing paper and any consignment of marble destined for St Paul's would also include a shipment of Genoa paper for the London printers.

While writing my ideas of how quickly the wreck broke up, made me think of how marble could be salvaged at the wreck site. I think the wreck was relatively intact for perhaps a week after her grounding. This would give an excellent opportunity to use the upright masts to unload some blocks from the hold. Perhaps up to 60 marble blocks were salvaged while the wreck lay grounded and before she broke up. Once the wreck collapsed, her own masts with block and tackle could not be used to salvage any more marble. Thus as soon as the masts went overboard, marble would have to be recovered using divers and a tidal lift. My new theory being 60 or more marble blocks were unloaded from the Bronze Bell wreck before it broke up. No further blocks were salvaged when it meant an underwater recovery.

There were not many merchant vessels as large as 700 tons in the year 1709. My guess throughout Europe there were less than fifteen merchant vessels trading of such a size which made me think it was going to be a relatively easy task to find her name. If this tonnage figure of 700 tons was not mentioned we could assume from the number of cannon on the ship and the tonnage of marble blocks carried the ship was a merchant one of at least 400 tons.

The ship is unlikely to be a naval ship as the names and losses of all those are well documented throughout the centuries. Naval ships had twice as many armaments compared to merchant ships. They also carried three times the crew and were not designed or constructed to take cargo. Naval ships were specifically for War, not for trading and carrying merchant goods.

What did the Bronze Bell ship look like ?

'Shipwrecks in the Americas' by Robert F. Marx would give approximate details of a 1680 ship of 700 ton ship. Dimensions; 102 ft (31 metres) length of keel. Beam 36.7 feet Draft 14.8 feet. With five or six anchors. He mentions that in 1688 a Fourth Rate British Man of War of 700 ton was required to have six anchors with an aggregate weight of 5.5 tons. Thus there are at least two anchors missing from the site, possibly salvaged from the site in April 1709. Wessex Archaeology confirm that the site dimensions are similar to the above with 37 metres of assumed wreck site length. With such a large ship it means that transporting any size of marble block is so much easier. Ragusan ships were renowned for being large and good cargo carriers. The size of ship meant that it could be well armed which also meant a large complement of men on board. Firing cannon at sea required at least four men to one cannon. The Bronze Bell Ship carried about 30-34 cannon meaning 10 or 12 gun ports on each side with a further 4 cannon at her stern and swivel guns on the poop deck. When looking at pictures of large ships with gun ports of this era the ones with two rows of gun ports will be Frigates or Men O' War. The ones having one line of gun ports and a cargo hold beneath are the armed merchantmen.

Imagine the above vessel but twice the size and that is what the Bronze Bell Ship would have looked like. A large three-masted vessel, buff bowed but carrying three square sails on her fore and main masts, with a lateen sail on her mizzen mast. She would carry at least 80 crew and a further 50 bombardiers and soldiers. I surmise that the crew consisted of Genoese sailors with perhaps military soldiers of a different nationality such as Italian. It would make sense that they were heading for Dublin with their London cargo, as there was more of an acceptance of Catholics in Ireland.

In Northern waters the Dutch had some of the largest vessels. In the Mediterranean when she was built in 1677, our ship would have been one of the largest merchant vessels afloat. .

Australia has built a full size replica of James Cook's sailing ship **HMS Endeavour.** The Bronze Bell ship was eighty years earlier but had similar dimensions.. **HMS Endeavour** replica is the closest vessel that can be seen afloat today that would look anything like the Bronze Bell Ship. When the replica **HMS Endeavour,** was constructed in 1994 she was made with 30 kilometres of rigging, has 750 wooden blocks or pulleys, and 28 sails that spread 10,000 square feet in canvas. She has a gross tonnage of 397 tons, a length of 33.3 metres, a waterline length of 30.9 metres, and a beam of 8.89 metres. Ignore the tonnage as being a lot less than the Bronze Bell. Naval burthen and merchant tonnage are different. If the original **HMS Endeavour** was measured as a merchant ship she would be the same tonnage as the Bronze Bell Ship.

The replica **HMS Endeavour**, Lieutenant James Cook's ship of 1797 has similar hull dimensions to the Bronze Bell Ship. This is the one of the few wooden ship replicas sailing today that would look anything like our ship. She carried a crew of 94.

When the ship was built in 1677, it was a watershed time for many of the Powers around the Adriatic and Italian coast. In 1670 the Venetian island of Crete was lost to Turkey. Venice was losing control of many of its Greek islands, and it was no longer the maritime influence it used to be. Dutch ships and English ones were taking over much of the Mediterranean trade. Spanish dominance of southern Italy and Sicily was weakening. The Republic of Genoa and the Republic of Ragusa strived hard to keep their independence allowing them to trade with everyone. Genoa had a strong trading export with England and it was a prime commercial centre for British Trade. The banks were run by Jewish interests who were made rich by loaning money to Spain. Genoa ships were hired out to foreigners, this meant that that the hirer could use the flag of Genoa and reduce the risk of being captured by corsairs. When marble was exported other cargoes would include wine, oil and paper. My original thoughts about a wine cargo on the Bronze Bell Wreck associated the lack of glass or pots seen on the wreck site. I then realised that this was probably transported in wooden casks or barrels. All evidence of which will be long gone to degradation by the sea.

Many of the large Croatian built ships were named **Argosy**, and indeed this ship may have had this name as well. At Cors y Gedol there is a table with an "A" carved into it. One of the pewter plates from the wreck site has the letter "A" inscribed into it. There is a strong possibility that the ship's name or the family name of the owner commenced with this letter. The Dubrovnik galleon *Argosy* is mentioned in two Shakespeare's plays: "Merchant of Venice" and "Taming the Shrew". The date of these is 1592, seventy five years before our Bronze Bell ship was built.

This name was so iconic for Ragusan vessels that the name of **"Argos"** or **"Argosy"** would have always been the choice name for a succession of Ragusan vessels over the decades. It is unfortunate that the bell does not reveal the name of the ship. Ships names on bells commenced about one hundred years later.

Bronze Bell Wreck   TOM BENNETT

How many cannon seen at the wreck site?

Wessex Archaeology wrote the most definitive report on the site in 2006. This report can be seen on the http://www.wessexarch.co.uk/files/splash-import/wp-content/uploads/2007/05/tal-y-bont-full-report-final-versionfigs_jan06.pdf . The report mentions earlier reports and measurement of cannon conducted by Sid Wignall in 1979. Twenty six guns were seen by Wessex Archaeology on the site in 2006. Many European naval vessels were armed with 40 guns or more. Like today Naval vessels did not carry merchandise. A naval ship would have its fate better recorded so that alone can rule out a British or French naval vessel.

In 1986 there were known to the Gwynedd Archive Service three swivel guns, one Saker cannon and an additional swivel gun being restored at the Armoury Department at the Tower of London. Most of these can now be seen at the Ty Gwyn Museum. This makes five known to be recovered by the Museum authorities. Wessex Archaeology in 2006 saw 26 guns on the seabed, but this only adds up to 31, when all previous estimates were for 34 plus guns.

The easiest guns to salvage are the swivel guns because of their smaller size and weight.

Tony Iles believes that the swivel guns were all made at the same foundry and can be dated to 1460 to 1490. There is a strong suggestion that they were made in France as they are similar to other swivel guns found on three other wreck sites. He is also of the opinion that they do not belong to the Bronze Bell Ship but belong to an earlier wreck. Three reasons support this. Firstly they appear to be below the marble mound. One swivel gun has not been recovered as it is below a marble block and remains in situ to show future archaeologists of how it could belong to another wreck. The scatter of swivel guns suggest another wreck lying in a more North/South orientation. The dates of the guns are two centuries earlier than the Bronze Bell wreck date. A ship as large as 700 tons would not have half a dozen small old guns as ballast. All the swivel guns were loaded with lead shot ready for action. These were not not acting as ballast in the bilges.

Sydney Wignall (1922-2012) Executive Director of the Atlantic Charter Maritime Archaeological Foundation is more well known for his Welsh Himalayan expedition and surveys of two Spanish Armada Ships, one in Blasket Sound, Ireland and one on Fair Isle. He was also interested in the **Bonhomie Richard** off Yorkshire and Francis Drake's lead coffin in Puerto Bello, Panama. He and his diving team had a good time, discovered 26 other shipwrecks but failed to find the one they were looking for. At that time I had ideas to mount diving expeditions but realized it was extremely difficult to obtain the finances to do so. One idea was to locate the lost land cannon of the Last Invasion of Britain, off the Carreg Wastad coastline near Fishguard. A Bicentenary of the event was coming up and I thought it a great idea to find artefacts from a longboat that had capsized when the French army were landing in 1797. The methodology for funding, was to first find the cannon, then apply for funding to locate and lift it. Then with one known success, I may be able to get sponsors for me to search for the lost bell of St David's Cathedral. Curiously, I did find the lost cannon but did not proceed with my plan as the Last Invasion Bicentenary celebrations came and went. I did not touch the cannon, but left it alone on the seabed, no-one else knowing of its discovery. I certainly was not going to inform CADW who would instantly slap an Historic Wreck order on the location and prevent any non-qualified underwater archaeologist from going near the place. Over the years I actually forgot about its existence. A few years ago Red Dragon Divers, the local sub aqua club, were telling me of their find of a wreck of about 1797, not far away. They have been dealing with the museum authorities and are a responsible group of divers. I told them of my little secret. In two summers they have failed to relocate this cannon lost in 1797 and lost again in 1976. Hopefully they will find it and it will be lifted and conserved with museum assistance, then to be displayed with the Invasion Tapestry at Fishguard Town Hall.

Bronze Bell Wreck   TOM BENNETT

This research has given me a better understanding of what may have happened in 1709. The ship itself was built around the year 1677, the date on the bell. Although the ship was owned by a Genoese Merchant, she may have been built in Croatia, I believe in the area twenty miles north of Dubrovnik.

Marble and paper was ordered by Lord Godolphin, to be shipped from the Republic of Genoa. Blocks of white Carrara marble were cut to specific sizes to form floor tiles or an altar platform, together with statue size blocks. The ship, with no name ascribed to her, was chartered by the British Government to convey the marble to Dublin. The blocks were loaded at Leghorn and packages of paper were loaded above. The vessel set sail between 26th December 1708 and 10th January 1709 from Genoa Bay. Although the weather was bitterly cold, the ship made good progress out of the Mediterranean and northwards through Bay of Biscay. Off the entire coastline of France, there were squadrons of French Frigates, Men O' War and Corsairs that were capturing merchant ships destined for London and holding them for ransom. One reason why the Bronze Bell ship is so large is that she could carry 30 cannon and a heavy cargo. The crew would be acquainted with lifting heavy guns on board and so lifting marble blocks of 1½ tons was not difficult. Even though the Bronze Bell ship had soldiers and armaments, they were wary of being captured so were taking their cargo to Dublin. With strong winds and no noon sight to make a fix the ship sailed north from Portugal for six days. Estimated voyage time from Leghorn to Dublin about 24-26 days. She entered the Irish Sea but met her first sighting of land was North Wales not the Irish coast. Once in Cardigan Bay, with any prevailing winds, ships get trapped and cannot escape. Sarn Badrig was not on any charts at that time. The ship could have holed herself on Sarn Badrig and in a sinking state was run for the beach. There is an inner channel where the ship was wrecked but wether the Captain was trying to negotiate this or was trying to deliberately run her onto the beach we cannot tell. His luck ran out. The ship grounded on a small isolated underwater rock some 400 meters from the beach. .

Try as they might, the ship would not get off the rock and with the swell and tidal range her hull was soon pierced. The marble blocks protruding through the broken hull into the reef, pegged the ship into a fixed position. Throwing paper cargo overboard did nothing to help get the stricken ship off the rock. The ship remained upright her decks awash at high water but her mast and rigging still intact. As the ship had not broken up and the crew not abandoned her, there was no loss of life amongst the 130 on board. Local men were soon on the scene to help. They managed to rescue those that wanted to come ashore. The Captain, realizing that possessions and some of the cargo could be salvaged if they worked quickly, obtained the services of local boats. In the next few days all the paper and at least eleven marble blocks were hoisted using the ship's booms, stays and derricks into boats alongside. These were taken to Barmouth where they were transferred into a Dublin trading vessel. Within a fortnight, probably the next Spring Tide, the weather turned nasty and the ship fell apart, her masts toppled and the wreck became completely submerged. From that point onwards the marble blocks lay in a mound on the reef, all more than 23 feet below the surface. It was no longer an easy task to retrieve more blocks so they remained there for two and a half centuries until discovered in the 1970's.

The crew were probably from the Republic of Genoa. They had landed on the shores of Wales when they were hoping to land in Ireland. Nevertheless, although Catholic in nature, they were not hostile enemies requiring capture, which would have been the case if they were French. It is thought that the captain and survivors would have sought passage back to Genoa or Leghorn on the next available merchant ship. These were regularly departing from Dublin and London, almost every six weeks. Some domestic items from the wreck and its timbers found their way into Cors y Gedol. It is likely that those at the mansion, provided hospitality for the crew and their repatriation expenses.

The blocks of marble and the salvaged paper would have been shipped from Barmouth to Dublin and then to London . The passage time to sail from Barmouth to Dublin would be a day and a half. Then it would take about seven days to sail to London. The printers in London, did get some of their ordered paper. Marble was stored at Scotland Yard and on 11th April 1709 an order was given to Wren to move eight pieces to Blenheim House, and a further three pieces to construct the Queen's Statue at St Paul's. This would mean the blocks were transported during the month of March, from Dublin to London and would not have been stored for very long in Scotland Yard.

Queen Anne statue at St Paul's, thought to be from marble salvaged from the Bronze Bell Wreck site in 1709. Can you see the pigeon?

If the Queen Anne's statue has marble from the Bronze Bell Ship then the sinking happened mid February to mid March 1709.

While thinking about the sequence of events after the grounding of the wreck, it now seems pretty clear that not only were some blocks salvaged before the wreck broke apart but that no subsequent salvage was ever done using diving operations.

Anchors at the site.

Three anchors and the broken remains of another one are present on the wreck site. Originally, the presence of these at either end of the site was one reason why some thought there may be two wrecks. I remember talking to the Cae Nest group in 1979 and suggested that a large vessel like the Bronze Bell Ship could have up to seven on board. The anchors seen are small in comparison to the tonnage of vessel. They are more kedge size and not the main bower anchors. No large anchors have been seen on the site or nearby. This fact suggests to me that the ship did not break up quickly and that no underwater operations were carried out. If a ship when sailing is suddenly grounded on a flat reef of boulders, she is carrying all her anchors. A ship in a storm as a last desperate measure may deploy anchors if it looks like she is going to be driven ashore. Also in storm conditions, the captain may deliberately run the ship ashore, thus carrying all her anchors. This ship being so large may not even deploy anchors at the last minute to keep the bows into the surf. Out of the above scenario, I think the ship was sailing when she grounded and it was fair weather, but with a big swell. On grounding the Captain will immediately order the sails to be backed to try to sail her backwards off the reef. This failing, one large bower anchor would be dropped. This would be standard practise even if they do not want to maintain their position on the reef. The bow is made much lighter and if the vessel floats she is not going move into any worse a position. The other bower anchor is probably taken by longboat to seaward into deeper water. Should the hull lift off the reef she can be hauled out to sea as the sails are set. When it was realized that the ship was not going to be extracted from the reef, it would be an easy operation to retrieve the anchor cables and lift the two bower anchors. The anchor cables could be grappled for, cut at the surface and lifted alongside a small boat and taken to Barmouth. This may have been done by local fishing men a year after the wrecking, and does not require a diver. This is why no large anchors are seen at the wreck site, they were salvaged over 200 years ago.

These photograph are from the Wessex Archaeology Report and shows the Kedge anchor situated at the extreme West (stern end) of the wreck site. This appears in remarkable condition for an anchor of this age in such an exposed position. The large flukes make for good holding in sand, mud and silt. Kedging is usually done to get a vessel out of a harbour where these substratum conditions exist.
The shank is 3.3 meters (10.8 feet long) .

Plate 4a: WA02: Anchor

To understand old anchors, *A Treatise on Ship's Anchors, by Cotsell 1856,* and the *.History and Development of English Anchors ca.1550 to 1850. Jobling, H.J.W Thesis,1993.* both available *as* free e-books. Essential reading for any diver or archaeologist.

This anchor is in the garden of Anchor House, Hoeten, near Dale in Pembrokeshire. It shows a larger shank (19 ft) than the Bronze Bell anchors, but similar proportions and is thought to be from a large merchant ship lost mid 18th Century. The ring is of a similar size to the anchor rings found on the Bronze Bell wreck and are made for the largest rope, 19 inch diameter, cables at the time.

Two anchors on the extreme East end of the wreck site lie together in the same position as they would if lashed to the hull as two Bower anchors on the starboard side of the ship. This, and the fact that more armaments are to be seen at the West end of the site indicate the bow and stern orientation of the wreck.

A Dutchman in 1678 wrote a treatise of Anchors stating that the length of the shank should be 4/10th the beam of the vessel. Using this calculation the three anchors on the site of about 3.3 metres length suggest a beam for our ship of 8.5 m maximum. However even ships of 600 ton would have a beam more like 9 metres.

As a quick and easy rule of thumb for divers looking for treasure in the Caribbean it was always the 'longer the shank the older the anchor, the sharper the V of the arms the more likely hood a Spanish Galleon'.

The anchor dimensions of the three complete anchors (minus wooden stocks) seen on the site are of similar weights and do not seem to be large enough for a ship of 700 tons. I have not seen the size of the flukes on the secondary bower anchors but assume they are not as large as seen on the kedge anchor. In the Mediterranean trade, anchors are needed to cut through sea grass weed rather than hold on a rocky substratum, thus the fluke and angle of arms are different to anchors seen on Northern trading waters of the Baltic and UK.

French anchors at the time had very rounded palm, adopted later by the British. However the V is not as pointed as seen on Spanish Galleons, that also had long and thin shanks on their anchors. I had a 45 ft yacht that had three large anchors and two small kedge anchors . Because the yacht had cruised in Greece and Turkey one anchor was specifically designed for the Eastern Mediterranean to hold better in eelgrass and soft silt. Like the ship's bells made in Spain in the 17th Century, the Spanish did not make good anchors despite having the best quality iron ore at the time.

Dead-eyes .

The fact that no wooden block pulleys or dead-eyes have been seen at the wreck site makes me think that the rigging, cordage and sheets were systematically removed from the wreck. A ship that is wrecked quickly, where the rigging is immersed and remains attached to the hull often presents hundreds of dead-eyes on a wreck site. They are easily recognisable objects for divers, but have not been mentioned in surveys. Invariably made of Lignum Vitae, the wood is so dense that it does not float and is not eaten by underwater fauna. The scarcity of these items at the wreck site indicates that these and pulley blocks were removed from the ship at the time of wrecking but before she sank.

When the replica **Endeavour** was made over 700 pulleys and dead-eyes were used; not one has been recorded at the Bronze Bell site.

Model of Man O' War **HMS Prince** showing her carrying two large Bower anchors on each side of her bow.

Photograph © Science Museum, London.

This is a contemporary model of a First Rate Man O' War **HMS Prince,** 1,200 ton burthen, built at Chatham just seven years before the Bronze Bell Ship was built. *Photograph © Science Museum, London.* The model shows two large Bower anchors secured in place on either side of the bow. This is the position of them lashed to the ship's hull when sailing. This vessel was a similar size to the Bronze Bell ship and the rigging would be similar. This was a Naval vessel of 100 guns, it would not take cargoes but was built to carry 300-400 men, with all their food supplies, arsenal and armaments It is thought the Bronze Bell Ship carried a large Bower anchor and a secondary anchor on each side of the bow. These are sometimes referred to as the Best Bower and the Small Bower. Usually the Best Bower is the largest of the anchors (unless a Sheet Anchor is carried in the bilges for emergencies) The Best Bower is always attached to an anchor cable in readiness for dropping.   Three anchors and the remains of a fourth are found on the wreck site. The anchor at the Western end of the wreck site would be a stern kedge anchor. The broken remains may be part of one of the Best Bowers but this does not seem much bigger than the secondary bower anchor. The above model shows both Bower anchors of a similar size. The wreck site lacks at least two anchors which I think were salvaged soon after the ship was wrecked. The fact that anchors and cannon are still on the seabed at all is an indication that no underwater salvage using divers was ever carried out. Bronze cannon were regarded as something extra special and these and the anchors at the site would have been salvaged if a diving team was present. An anchor prior to 1815 had a large wooden stock (cross piece) made from two large pieces of oak banded together. Although shanks remain, wooden stocks are rarely seen on wreck sites. Before 1811, anchors were tied to anchor hawsers, large fibre ropes which meant a large iron ring was fitted to the top of the shank. At the beginning of the 19th Century anchor chain cables and all-iron anchors commenced to be used. Wooden stocks were replaced with iron stocks. Large attachment rings were replaced with smaller rings for anchor chain to be shackled.

This extremely accurate pencil drawing shows the bow section of a
Dutch Man O' War getting ready to sail to London to defeat the English
fleet in the Thames. Drawn by Willem Van De Velder the Elder about
the same date as the Bronze Bell Ship was built. It shows two wooden
stock anchors being lashed to the starboard quarter. In the northern
hemisphere because of the anticlockwise nature of wind in storms, the
starboard anchor was always let go first. Here the two Bower anchors
are about the same size and it is the aft one that is tied to the anchor
cable. Ships built before 1700 were commonly seen with a "Beak" at
the bow. The front of the ship was known as the "Heads" the toilet area
for the crew. A nautical term still used today.

The accuracy of the chart entry giving a tonnage of 700 tons has not
been doubted. The Wessex Archaeology Report considered the anchors
seen were undersized for a 700 ton ship. I am suggesting that the
anchors indicate a ship of 480 to 600 tons, which is still a sizeable ship.
If the British Government was chartering the ship, the ship would be
carrying appropriate anchors for the size of ship. This implies William
Morris had overestimated the size that was entered on the chart. He is
said to have been friends with the Vaughans so he is unlikely to have a
tonnage wildly incorrect. It was forty years later when the chart
information was added.

During this time ships, especially merchant ships were generally much larger. He perhaps knew it may be nearer to 600 tons but gave the higher tonnage as that would emphasise the large size for its time of sinking. I have been told that he was close friends with the Vaughans. If the ship had been assigned a name the Vaughans would undoubtedly have made a record of it. They would also have knowledge of the name of the master and the tonnage of the vessel. If, as I suggest, the ship was chartered with no name, then no name could be given to Morris for his chart entry. By no exact tonnage being given may suggest that the vessel being chartered was the ex San Antonio, where naval tonnage or burthen was not generally recorded. Naval vessel were classified as so many guns, in the San Antonio case this was 34 guns. Morris was not going to put 34 guns on the chart as it would imply a naval vessel which it was not.

There has been identified an anchor fluke of a slightly larger size amongst the cargo heap which has broken with the associated shank totally missing. This is an unusual event. Anchors only break under exceptional load which is usually applied laterally. My theory is that soon after grounding this anchor was deliberately placed under the amidships part of the hull to act as a prop to hold the vessel upright. It a clever plan by the Captain to stop the ship from falling over at low tide. It helps in adding time to both evacuate and to extract cargo using the in situ masts. This broken off fluke is larger than those seen on the other anchors and thus more suitable in British waters. Even if not much heavier than the two other anchors remaining in the bow area of the wreck site it is considered that this was one of the Bower anchors.

When the wreck finally collapsed the weight of the marble in the hold together with the remaining hull weight and water pressure fell onto this anchor breaking it apart. The hull fell over on top of this anchor. As the anchor hawser cable was still attached to this broken anchor it was a simple matter to recover it from the surface, leaving just the fluke on the seabed.

An anchor of this size does not completely deteriorate and disappear even after being in shallow oxygen rich water for 300 years. The sharp composite pieces of a wrought iron anchor shank usually remain.

Because this broken part of the anchor lies beneath one of the cargo blocks, suggests that the anchor was lying on the seabed before the 1709 cargo arrived. Could this be an indication of another vessel already lying there before Bronze Bell Ship or merely an individual lost anchor from a previous time?

However if we look at the size of anchors still remaining they relate more to a vessel of 500 tons. Even that is a large merchant ship for that time. Using data from English anchors in Joblings Thesis, the anchors seen at the wreck site are more in keeping with a merchant ship of 480 tons and a maximum length of 86 feet (26 m). Wessex Archaeology report suggest the wreck could be 28 feet (8.5 m) more than this. It must be remembered that measuring a ships length is not an exact science. From beak to stern or on deck measurements or keel length are all going to be a different length figure. This is when the ship is intact, once broken up on the seabed the bow and stern could fall outwards making further inaccuracies in estimating the ship's length. The beam of a wreck site, being about one quarter of the length is a far more accurate and easier measurement to take. It is also a more relevant measurement. Some of the ways of calculating the size of anchors needed was based on beam of the ship. Thus working backwards from anchor and fluke sizes, the beam of the vessel and hence its approximate tonnage can be found.

Reasons for ship losses at St Patrick's Causeway/ Sarn Badrig.
Just south of the Lleyn Peninsular at the northern end of Cardigan Bay
is a large natural corner. All ships destined for Liverpool and Glasgow
have to pass this area. The bay is shaped like a huge net to catch
any sailing vessels unfortunate to get caught there in the prevailing
South Westerlies. In bad weather sailing vessels get driven there by
Westerly winds. As well as the shape of the coastline the area poses
other hazards. Strong ebb tides off Bardsey Island, cause slow moving
sailing vessels difficulties in rounding the headlands to get to the shelter
of Holyhead. They are then forced to return to the Pwllheli area. The
whole area of Cardigan Bay has few natural features making navigation
difficult. Captains in 1700 would have to rely on previous knowledge of
a navigator who had been there before or an accompanying ship that
had someone on board who knew the area. There were no accurate
charts of the area. Stretching out into the bay for some ten miles is a
reef of boulder rocks, that many unsuspecting captains have found to
their cost. It is a rocky terminal moraine from the last Ice Age and is so
shallow that ships of any size can hit it. Parts of the reef can be seen at
Low Water Springs and there is nowhere else around the British
coastline that has a similar hazard. Navigators in unfamiliar areas,
have to take certain things for granted. They look along the coast and
estimate if there are likely to be offshore rocks or islands. If they think
it is safe they would take depth soundings and sail three to four miles
away from the land, skirting the coast. If this was done in north
Cardigan Bay, even in settled weather a ship would invariably hit Sarn
Badrig, The captain and navigator would be completely unaware of an
unusual reef lurking south westward for more than ten miles out to sea.
Once stranded, because of the depth and harsh boulders, the ship was
unlikely to be got off. Most of the losses are ships travelling northward.
There is even a tidal set on the flood tide that takes ships into this part
of Cardigan Bay. For ships outward bound from Scotland, the Clyde
and Liverpool, Sarn Badrig posed no hazard. Taking a course direct
from Bardsey Island to Strumble Head or The Smalls would avoid the
hazard of Sarn Badrig.

There are numerous instances of vessels sailing north from the Portuguese coast intending to enter the English Channel but find themselves off the Pembrokeshire coast. In bad weather or fog, navigators could not obtain their noon or star sights because of cloud cover. They were forced to rely on Dead Reckoning, the distance run on their logs, I.e., ship's speed and compass direction. Commonly they entered a northern channel some fifty miles further on than the English Channel. This was the Bristol Channel and referred to as the "False Channel". With days of continuous gales the South Westerlies would take unsuspecting ships into Cardigan Bay. To survive hurricane force winds, as happened in November 1703, a ship to survive can only go with the gale and run the entire length of the Irish Sea hoping the wind will die down before they meet the coast of Scotland. Other vessels venturing into the north end of Cardigan Bay, by stress of weather, compass error or tidal set find themselves on Sarn Badrig or a lee shore near Pwllheli.

There is the little known fact of compass error that can cause ships to be navigated West of the Isles of Scilly. When any ships set sail from the Mediterranean or from places like Brazil, they should first swing or reset the ship's compass and make a Compass Correction Chart. Ships made of iron or carrying a lot of iron ore or even cannon, over the period of an Atlantic crossing or two weeks sailing from the Mediterranean, can become magnetized. The ship itself is magnetised like a large compass, making a few degrees error on different points of sailing. This causes, over a few weeks, even more deviation than that already known in the ships compass. More error than the recent Correction table would show. All Deviation must be corrected to know where Compass North and hence True North lies. Although the captain would have been reliant on a navigator with previous knowledge rather than any chart. A corrected compass is essential. An accurate compass, distance run with the log, and noon sights of the sun to determine Latitude, would all be needed to find the English Channel or Dublin, even for a skilled navigator.

Today with gyro and fluxgate compasses and GPS navigation is used we forget the difficulties involved in navigation and the reliance that sailors had on a traditional magnetic compass. The navigators had to use their knowledge of their vessel and every scrap of experience. Merchant Captains often stayed a lifetime with the same vessel. Some would know that in the prevailing Westerlies once they left Lisbon on the Portuguese coast they could sail keep sailing due North and the leeway made by the wind would keep them on a rhumb line for Kinsale, Ireland. A rhumb line meaning a course using a constant compass direction. In clear weather when the North Star could be seen this could be achieved without an accurate compass. However, in overcast weather, stars are hidden by clouds, and no proper sextant sights can be made. Sun sights at noon to work out Longitude is not possible or sufficiently accurate with cloud cover. We have to remember that although navigation was a science there was also a lot of luck or bad luck involved. Only two years before the best navigators of the British Navy, together with Admiral Sir Cloudesley Shovell and four Men O' War were completely lost on the Isles of Scilly. It was from that time onwards that Longitude and ships time pieces made for more accurate navigation. Before that the log distance run and the course steered were the principle factors to obtain an Estimated Position. For the Bonze Bell Ship Captain there were no lighthouses en route, to warn of hazards and to guide. The Smalls Lighthouse was not built and lit for another 66 years.

There are additional problems with compasses in the Irish Sea. Not identified and not known in 1700. Chris Holden's book on North Wales Shipwrecks mentions such in the wreck of the **Duncan** in 1914. This steam-trawler ran onto the reef in due to an uncorrected compass and the fact that the Causeway Buoy light had failed. However, a report from 1847 suggests that there were known problems with magnetic compasses in this area. When you are within a cable's length of the shallow edge of the Sarn Badrig, the compass is observed to be much affected, turning sometimes quite round, and varying in every direction, yet at a distance of two cable's length, it becomes right again, and points as usual. *Seaman's New Guide. 1847.*

Two cables is not very far, only 372 metres. A cable length is equal to one tenth of a nautical mile or approximately 100 fathoms. The unit is named after the length of a ship's anchor cable in the Age of Sail. When anchor cables were made of chain, they had joining links in them every one cable. $\frac{1}{10}$ nautical mile, or 185.2 metres to one cable. The normal rule when anchoring is that the scope (length let out) should be at least three times the depth of water. Thus with a standard cable most ships could anchor theoretically in 100 metres of water, in practice they sought about 10 to 20 metres depth to anchor. Maximum depth in Cardigan Bay is around 50 metres and near to Sarn Badrig about 20 metres.

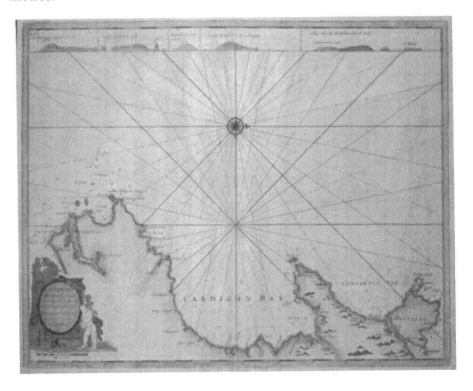

One of the first charts of Cardigan Bay, printed 40 years after the Bronze Bell Ship was wrecked, still does not show Sarn Badrig. Later charts were drawn with north uppermost.

Bronze Bell Wreck   TOM BENNETT

I remember seeing a yacht, one of the survivors of the Fastnet gale, a few days after the storm in 1979 sailing carefully down the Welsh coastline off Cardigan. He was obviously looking for the safety of Fishguard Harbour after having sensibly abandoned the race and run up or been driven up the Irish Sea with the hurricane behind him to get out of trouble. He ended up 160 miles north of his intended rhumb line. Likewise in the Red Sea, having spent all night weathering a storm and getting no sleep I then decided to run before it and ended up 80 miles in the wrong direction! These are just two examples of what can happen in modern times with sailing vessels in a storm. Both had efficient navigation systems, but were physically driven off their intended course. It is thought the Captain of the Bronze Bell Ship was unfamiliar with Cardigan Bay, and had not intended to be there. However he could have been experienced and had noticed the breaking water over Sarn Badrig and was avoiding the reef. This implies that it was not storm conditions or at night when hitting the reef is almost inevitable. By the time the reef is seen it is often too late to take avoiding action. A cautious captain, even in fair weather, would have men continually throwing out the lead line to take soundings of the depth. He may have noticed the shallow Causeway and had seen an area of sea with no breaking white water, so sailed towards it. There is sand either side of the reef and the boulders that he hit were only a meter higher than the seabed. This means however slowly he was sailing the log readings showed the ship to be safe, albeit in very shallow water. There is a six metre tidal range, a factor unfamiliar with Mediterranean captains. While sailing the tidal range is of little significance, and there were no charts to refer to. Once the ship had grounded the range is critical and makes a huge difference as to how quickly the ship can be refloated and how soon the hull is going to break apart. I suggest the ship hit mid tide, say three hours before Low Water, in fair weather say force 2 or 3. She grounded on a flat reef of rocks. The ship held fast. Within an hour or so her hull had pounded in the swell and some heavy marble blocks had spilled out of her broken hull. These blocks helped to keep the vessel in an upright position but also fast to the reef.

There are two churches close to Dyffryn Ardudwy beach that may reveal more in their burial records. One is Llanenddwyn church and the other Llanddwywau, (spelt Llanddwywe today). The second church has a private pew for the Vaughans of Cors y Gedol constructed inside the north chancel in 1615. Most consider that the wreck happened in severe conditions. If this were so there would have been a great loss of life. There would be at least 130 people on board. It would be unusual for them all to survive if the ship was driven onto a lee shore in gale force winds. Of those lost it is likely that eight out of ten bodies would be be washed ashore on the coastline. Local people were extremely superstitious of retrieving bodies from the shoreline. If the sea had taken a body, then you leave it alone, mentality. In those days if a drowned sailor was found, of unknown faith, they could be left to rot on the seashore or if buried, buried outside the consecrated ground of a church graveyard. This scenario is unlikely in the Bronze Bell Wreck. With survivors who could confirm they were of a Christian faith, the bodies would have been buried in the churchyards The majority of the crew were probably Catholic. The local Welsh people would not be particularly hostile to Catholics. If the wreck had happened on the south coast of England, it would be a far different matter. When a great number of Catholics arrived unexpectedly on the coast they were quickly sent home again. As far as I have been told the church records do not show any persons being buried in 1709 and the State Records are silent on the wreck. This implies that there were no deaths and the ship may not have broken up quickly like we may assume from it position on a lee shore. I am sure that if more than ten deaths had occurred, the wreck would be more prominent in local folklore. Mass burials were common near to the shoreline if a large number of bodies needed to be buried. When 63 men and 3 women required burial in November 1760 from the wreck of the **Caesar** near Pwlldu Head, Gower, the Captain was forced to pay the local people to dig a common grave on the nearest available piece of land. No such story exists of a mass grave near to Dyffryn Ardudwy.

Some of the Bronze Bell Ship survivors are thought to have settled locally. Two years after the event there are some baby Baptisms in Towyn Merionethshire in 1713 and 1714 that hint of Italian or foreign names. EVANUS AP EVAN 1714 Gulielmi Elizabeth at Tywyn GRACE (child's name) DAVID 1715 Gulielmi Catherine at Llancyl. DAVID DAVID 1715 Gulielmi Joane at Twyn. HUGO EDWARD 1715. Gulielmi at Ffestiniog JANA EDWARD 1715 Ludovici Catherine at Twyn. WYN JOHES EDWARD 1713 Ludovici Anna at Twyn

We have no records about Gulielmi being used as first name. So one assumes the scribe is referring to the name Gwilym as it occurs a lot in the Baptism records. Surname Gulielmi is used at least 13 times in at least 5 counties. What is perhaps more relevant is the father's name of Ludovici Edward in 1713 who with his wife Anna was Baptizing their daughter Johes Edward at Towyn. The name Juan Benedictus, of Italian origin, known to be buried locally in 1730, could have been a survivor of the wreck. His surname has been suggested as the source of the Bennett Williams families in the area. The Bennett part is my own surname and I know my own ancestors were from mid Wales, but had originally come from Cornwall. I would like to think that I was associated with a survivor of the Bronze Bell Wreck but I am rather sceptical. The name Bennett was already in existence for two generations around the Wales coast, and for a much longer time in the Tin mines near Redruth in Cornwall. There was a Bennett, a mining engineer specializing in water extraction that moved from Cornwall to Ffestiniog around this time. The Bennett that begat the Bennett Williams family may also have spawned the Bennett Jones family name in Ffestiniog. They could have descended from either the Benedictus or the Cornish mining engineer. A few of the Bronze Bell Crew, with Italian surnames, seem to have integrated into the Llandudwy community. With a pre-eminently Catholic crew it would be interesting to know whether many more of the crew settled in Dublin in March 1709.

Name of Ship.
No name has been found for this ship, despite many weeks of looking through documents and news of the day. If any name can be suggested it is **Argosy**. The name was used at the time for a merchant ship built in Ragusa and was used by Shakespeare.

An argosy is a merchant ship, or a fleet of such ships. As used by Shakespeare (e.g., in King Henry VI, Part 3, Act 2, Scene VI; in the *Merchant of Venice,* Act 1, Scene I and Scene III; and in The *Taming of the Shrew,* Act 2, Scene I), the word means a flotilla of merchant ships operating together under the same ownership. However Shakespeare existed one hundred years before this vessel was wrecked. The word Argosy is derived from the 16th century city Ragusa (now Dubrovnik, in Croatia), a major shipping power of the day and entered the language through the Italian ragusea, meaning a Ragusan ship. I have seen it written that the word bears no relation to the ship **Argo** from Greek mythology (Jason and the Argonauts). However I would have guessed otherwise.
Since "argosy" and "odyssey" sound alike and both refer to ships or voyage by ship. "odyssey" refers to Odysseus' journey, not to his ship, which goes unnamed in Homer's Odyssey. Occasionally "argosy" is misused as a synonym for "odyssey," namely as an adventure. The letter 'A' as seen on some artefacts is more than likely the first letter of the ship's name.
When researching possible ships of this size belonging to the Republic of Genoa, I came across another possibility. They had a **San Antonio**, A Fifth Rate Man O' War that they acquired in 1667 (Ie ten years before the bell date of 1677) It was sold by their Navy in November 1669. *Reference: Nomenclature des Navires Français de 1661 à 1715 Alain Demerliac* There are three factors of interest here. That this ship carried 34 guns in 1669, that its name begins with 'A' and that if she was our Bronze Bell ship it did not have a large cargo hold, hence only suitable for carrying 66 tons of marble. This ship, built as a naval ship may have been sold to a Genoese merchant who then hired the vessel out. The Bronze Bell could have replaced an earlier bell that was on the ship when decommissioned.

The fate of this **San Antonio** is not known, but her size (tonnage not known) would undoubtedly be of a similar size as the Bronze Bell Ship.

By the name not being known or remembered by the crew or local Welsh inhabitants suggests the following.
1. The name was deliberately kept secret, the British Government not wanting the port of Genoa to record a name on her departure, for fear of the ship being captured by the French and losing the marble cargo.
3. The ship was recently captured as a prize and had not been renamed.
4. The ship was chartered and no name assigned.

My assumption that we cannot find a name is that the ship was never assigned a name for it last voyage. The Genoese were skilled business men and their Jewish bankers more so. They were in the habit of chartering out their merchant vessels. If they called the ship a particular name it may jeopardise a potential client from wanting to hire the ship. The potential customer may dislike a certain name, or be prejudiced to the language it was written in. The intended customers were from all nationalities, covering more than 19 languages. Thus it was decided the best option was not to assign a ship's name at all. If the hirer, authority or company wished to designate a name of their choice, that was their prerogative. Some would be superstitious regarding a name change as being the forerunner of bad luck. This would not apply if the ship had no name in the first place. It would be as though it was being named for the first time.

This could still fit in with the **San Antonio**. A Genoese family/company could have purchased this ship in 1669 with the intention of hiring it out to France, Spain or Italy as and when they needed her. When the British come along and want 66 tons of marble delivered to Dublin in 1709 they could have chartered the same vessel. As the San Antonio was never designed to carry a cargo, this ship perhaps could only safely carry 66 tons, blocks stacked three high not in the lowest part of the hull.

As long as the ship could deliver the marble it would have suited the British very well. The established crew were accustomed to lifting guns and heavy objects the size of marble blocks. It was well armed with a neutral militia. All would be happy that the ship had no name at the commencement of the charter. As the Genoese company had more than one merchant vessel on their books, they, for convenience had to identify it by a number or a letter of the alphabet. As this was their largest or Number One merchant vessel the letter 'A' was ascribed to it. Objects belonging to the ship when it was named **San Antonio** may have had an 'A' on them. The Genoese company would assure the client that they could call the vessel whatever they liked, but for their own company the vessel was known as 'A'.

It can now be appreciated why a table from the ship and a platter both possessed the letter 'A'. This also sorts the oddity that the name of the ship was not handwritten onto the chart. Lewis Morris knew it had no name and thus said 'Genoese Ship'. The realization that no name had been found because no name was ever given, leaves me with the emotion of achievement but it is also something of an anti-climax. I feel somewhat cheated that I spend months searching for a name only to find that the ship never had a name allotted to her. What a B.....! (That is an abbreviation of Bronze Bell).

I have failed to find more about this **San Antonio,** but we know it was a Genoese ship with 34 guns that had been sold off by the navy in 1669. I do not even know if it was still sailing in 1709. If our Bronze Bell Ship the bell had been added later and the ship could be ten years older than previously thought. The **San Antonio,** was probably built in Genoa around 1667.

https://threedecks.org/index.php?display_type=show_ship&id=19918

Who was living at Cors y Gedol in 1709?

Richard Vaughan II , a prominent figure in North Wales politics and his wife Margaret, were living at the nearby Manor House of Cors y Gedol. Richard been brought up at the manor, was 44 years of age and had married his wife Margaret, nine years before. He was Sheriff of Merionethshire 1668-1669 and Sheriff of Caernarvonshire 1699-1700. From 1704 -1716 he was Constable of Harlech Castle. He died in 1734 having been a member of Parliament for 33 years without having to contest his seat. The Bronze Bell wreck landed on the shoreline not far from the Cors y Gedol and some items were salvaged from the wreck, notably a large table, silverware and pewter. From 1710, Vaughan was

less active in politics and spent a considerable time making renovations and extensions to the buildings at Cors y Gedol.

Gateway at Cors y Gedol was built in 1630 and was supposedly rebuilt or extended with timbers from the Bronze Bell wreck in 1710.

Richard Vaughan's eldest son William succeeded him at the Manor and also as a Tory in the constituency. The Vaughans would undoubtedly have written about the wreck in a daily diary. All gentry kept diaries, and these will be in existence today, possibly in the Vaughan Manuscripts. Around 1740 one of the Vaughans wrote that the Gate House at Cors y Gedol was designed by the Royal Architect Inigo Jones.(1573-1652)

Bronze Bell Wreck   TOM BENNETT

There are also stories of timbers from the wreck site being used in buildings at Cors y Gedol, the local manor house, which was extended by Richard II Vaughan after 1711. Richard Vaughan (1665-1734) was High Sheriff of Merionethshire in 1698, and Caernarvonshire 1699-1700. He was a Tory member of Parliament for 33 years and constable of Harlech Castle 1704-16. After 1710 he was less active at Westminster and was said to be spending more time fitting out his house with wall panelling and rebuilding. These dates do coincide with timbers coming from the wreck in 1709. In 1705 his religious persuasion was said to be "Low Church" i.e., Anglican Church that emphasizes evangelicalism and lays little stress on the sacraments, church rituals, and church authority.

I have to digress to tell you that Robert Vaughan (1606 -1636) was exceedingly bulky and corpulent (in other words fat). He was a Member of Parliament at the early age of 23 and they had to open the large doors, to let him in. MP's already seated, when they saw the big door being opened, used to exclaim "here comes the Black Rod or the Welsh Mayor!" He must have been one of the first to have fat removal surgery. The operation was not a success as he died shortly afterwards at Cors y Gedol in 1636.

The gateway at Cors y Gedol today.

Bronze Bell Wreck   TOM BENNETT

During the 15th Century a Griffith Vaughan built "Y Ty Gwyn in Bermo" where the Museum of the Bronze Bell is held. I had always assumed it was built by the Griffith Vaughan who was Sheriff of Merionethshire in 1677. However a contemporary 15th Century poem describes the building of three premises and confirms that Gruffydd Fechan (Vaughan) of Cors y Gedol built Ty Gwyn between 1460-1485. The Poem and its translation is to be seen on the website of the Sailors' Institute, Barmouth. This date is endorsed by the fact that in 1600, two Welsh poems mention that Ty Gwyn was in a state of disrepair.

In 1565, there were only four houses in Barmouth and Ty Gwyn (White House) was one of them. Many coastal cottages were whitewashed with lime in the Victorian era, when limekilns produced quick-lime for neutralising the soils. However to paint a structure white prior to 1600 meant only one thing. It was a beacon, like a lighthouse, to be seen by ships out at sea, a navigation mark to show sailors where Barmouth was. There was also an early tower or beacon, long since gone, directly in line with Ty Gwyn. When lined up as a transit, the two structures would direct ships over Barmouth bar into the estuary. It is now the oldest building in Barmouth appearing in any archive record. History has it that Jasper Tudor, spent a night in Ty Gwyn. Two dates are possibilities; in 1468 he landed in North Wales in an attempt to relieve Harlech Castle or it could have been October 1483. His uncle was the first Tudor king, Henry VII, who defeated Richard III at the Battle of Bosworth. The Griffith Vaughan responsible for building Ty Gwyn was married to Lowry, a niece of Owain Glyndwr.

The Bronze Bell Museum is housed in the upper part of Ty Gwyn. Gwynedd County Council and Gwynedd Archive Service have made the Museum possible with much dedication and volunteer work from a host of local residents. A thriving cafe "Davy Jones' Locker" is in the lower portion of the building. You must go there, so that you can boast you have had 'Tea at the White House' a Trump card for any visitor to Barmouth.

Ty Gwyn as we see
the building today.

Ty Gwyn when the sea
lapped at its footings in
1830.

Ty Gwyn is the building on the left of this picture. Note the
sloping roof, now above Davy Jones Locker, extended to join the
roof of the main building, giving a more pointed appearance to
the white painted South elevation. Engraved by Henry Adlard
(1799-1893) from an original study in 1830 by the topographical
painter Henry Gastineau. Look at the huge old anchor positioned
near the quay, mid foreground. It is massive, with no wooden
stock and could be one of the Bower anchors salvaged from the
Bronze Bell wreck, retrieved the century before. It is also resting on
top of a white stone block!

Bronze Bell Wreck   TOM BENNETT

Prior to 1999 an oil painting existed locally, the whereabouts now unknown. It was said to show the Bronze Bell wreck with its masts still upright and thought to be painted in 1709. If this painting is ever located, I am sure it would also show smaller boats alongside undergoing either evacuation of the crew or a salvage operation in place. Just like a news photograph today, somebody wanted to record the event, especially as they had never seen such a huge ship before. The existence of this painting gives credence to my theory that the ship did not break up quickly, but remained grounded long enough for some salvage to take place.

Barmouth in 1798. Engraved by John Walker (flourished 1784-1802) from an original drawing by Charles Catton (1756-1819). It is not known if Walker was responsible for adding the ships in the harbour and the fishing boats in the foreground but they are completely out of proportion to the rest of the etching. Behind the fisherman selling his fish is another anchor. This is a much smaller anchor and still shows its wooden stock and cable and has nothing to do with the larger anchor in the 1830 picture.

.

Barmouth in 1798.

This is the only picture, I have seen, which shows Ty Gwyn from a North Westerly direction Ie from where Ty Crwn (Round House) is now positioned, built 1833. What is of interest is the "chimney" on the Ty Gwyn roof. This structure may look like a tall chimney or bell tower but it has an opening on its West side as a place for a beacon light. Directly below it to the right of the rear steps is a rectangular wall painted white. This is the West elevation and was plainly visible for ships passing Barmouth sailing a few miles off the coast. Today other buildings block this view.

By this date at the end of the 18th century, a chart by the late Lewis Morris was available to help mariners navigate into Barmouth Harbour. The chart does not show any leading marks using Ty Gwyn and its white coloured walls. It does show two channels into the estuary, a North Bar and The Bar. The southern most channel called The Bar, is the wider and deeper channel and shows a Perch, a mast with a top mark on it. Once over the bar navigators could stay in the main channel by keeping South of the Perch ie leaving it to Port when entering. From the Perch, ships could sail East (into the estuary). Then, when they could see the front face of Ty Gwyn (a broad white arrow) they could turn towards it to find the Barmouth Quay and Beach.

Enlarged picture of the West elevation of Ty Gwyn on the 1798 picture. Not only is one wall painted white but the other wall in the strong midday sun (from the South) causes a shadow making an inverted triangle shape. This other wall in shadow making a black and white contrasting pattern triangle shape. This lean to structure must have been added to prevent the west wall from being seen by navigators when entering over the bar.

This painted wall was a mark to identify Barmouth to those out
at sea. The following diagram represents what the West facing wall of
Ty Gwyn would look like when a mile or two offshore. Ships passing
Barmouth in daytime would see a rectangular white shape beneath dark
mountains.

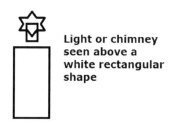

**Light or chimney
seen above a
white rectangular
shape**

If however ships are going North from Aberystwyth or Fishguard, they
will be approaching from the South and will not see any white wall until
they have already passed the estuary mouth. They would only see the
white painted surface of the front South elevation of the building, once
they have successfully entered the estuary This showed a larger arrow
and the roof of the structure now above Davy Jones Locker was built to
enhance the arrow direction. This roof used to continue at the same
angle as the main roof of Ty Gwyn to provide a larger expanse of front
elevation wall to be painted white. If a ship has sailed passed the
entrance and is due East of Barmouth the front elevation of Ty Gwyn
cannot be seen but the white rectangle then is prominently seen. I have
read somewhere that there used to be a tower at the back of the town,
long since removed, that added a leading transit with Ty Gwyn to enable
vessels to come over the Barmouth Bar in safety. By looking at a Chart
of the harbour entrance, the location of this back marker, a stone tower
on higher ground, should be easy to find. I surmise that the white
rectangle mark may have been useful for local vessels to navigate into
the North Channel but it could not be seen by vessels entering the Main
Channel.

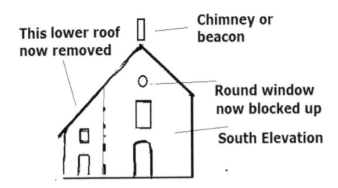

The elongated 'chimney' at the rear of the building when in line with the apex of the front gable, directs ships directly onto the beach below Ty Gwyn. To see this front elevation, ship would have to be approximately south of Ty Gwyn, therefore it may not have helped vessels outside the estuary, only those once safely inside the estuary. It must be remembered that this was at a time before harbours were built and ships needed to know where they could beach safely on sand.

Further South in Cardigan Bay in the 19th Century different shaped stone stone beacons were constructed for mariners to find the harbours of Porthgain and Abereiddy. These day-beacons were essential for finding these places when the coastline on either side is so indistinct when seen from a distance out at sea. My idea that the elongated 'chimney' at the rear of Ty Gwyn displayed a light at night is not verified. However a round window, now blocked up, on the front elevation may have displayed a light at night. Most estuaries with a sand bar would not be entered at night, unless with local knowledge. The channel is forever changing and large surf over it cannot be seen from the seaward side. Today all busy ports have leading marks or buoys for vessels to follow in daytime and leading lights to direct ship traffic down the correct shipping lanes at night. Transit marks, lining up two objects, to get a direction is extremely accurate. Having two sets at 90% to each other can pinpoint a position at sea easier than using a GPS phone. In the past I have painted my own white marks on the breakwaters at Fishguard to re-locate by transit wreck sites both inside and outside the harbour!

Early ship's bells.

The ship's name is not seen on the early ship's bells. Certainly not sixteenth century ones. All their casting marks are still visible and a date is usually given, albeit in Latin numerals prior to 1600.

Holding the bell onto a frame or support requires a ring or bracket with holes in it. This is an integral part of the bell and is called a canon, the head or the supporting ring. The canon on the top of the bell is often of a simple shape in the same plane, although it may have one or three holes (eyes) to secure it to a supporting frame, called the yoke. Spanish ship's tended to have canon with a triangular pattern. Venetian ship bells are known to have canon with three round holes. Other Spanish bells have been found on shipwrecks from a similar date to the Bronze Bell wreck also showing similar canon, implying similar yoke suspension. At the moment if the Bronze Bell wreck is Ragusan built with a Croatian bell then it is unique amongst known underwater sites. We may have to wait for more Mediterranean shipwrecks to reveal their bells before we have the opportunity to make comparisons with other Ragusan built vessels. This research indicates that Ragusan built vessels could be lying on the seabed around the UK coast or in the Baltic or anywhere around Europe. Two Venetian shipwrecks lie off the coast of Ireland. Relating bells found to shipwreck identification, brings up the responsibility of amateur divers when they find an unidentified shipwreck. Bells with ship's names on them, have always been the iconic artefact for divers to search for. The bell, is often the first and most important artefact that is discovered. If a bell is retained by the finder as a diving souvenir and is not properly photographed or its foundry markings or lettering not recorded, then future researchers will have lost many essential clues as to the identity of the vessel to which it belonged. All bells found are required by law to be declared to the Receiver of Wreck. www.gov.uk/government/groups/receiver-of-wreck

The photograph © Badewanne Oy is from a Dutch ship that sank in 1709, the same date as our wreck. The belfry was like a shrine on board the ship. Reverence and prayers were made to it and it was the heart and soul of the ship.

http://www.narhvalen.dk/mystery-18th-century-shipwreck-found-gulf-finland-documentation-reveals-pristine-details.

On top of each ship's bell is a protruding piece named a canon which has holes in it with which the bell is hung. The picture above shows a multifaceted canon, more typical of Dutch, naval or Baltic built ship. Compare to the more simple canon on the Bronze Bell. Early ship's bells were hung in a yoke and a belfry, just like Church Bells. Different countries and different foundries tended to have varying designs of canon. For comparison there are two other known bells. The **Sveti Pavao** Shipwreck, has a ship's bell dated 1567 and with a Venetian provenance from Mljet, Croatia . Another ship's bell from a Venetian trader is from a shipwreck site in the bay of Salandinak, shows a canon ring with three holes, The eyes or holes in the canon are similar in shape to the Bronze Bell. However the Bronze Bell canon ring is diamond and angular in shape whereas the **Salandinak Bell** has a very rounded shape above the holes.

I am sure the Bronze Bell was not cast in Spain for a variety of reasons. One being that the eye shapes are different. Spanish bells have a reversed triangular shaped canon ring as seen in the **Tortugas** Wreck and the **Western Ledge Reef** wreck. A late 17th Century bell made in Spain, that is found underwater invariably shows severe corrosion or cracking. Our bell shows no surface corrosion.

Bronze Bell 1677   Spanish Bell 1697

The above suspension rings or canon are both from Mediterranean merchant ships and at first sight show a similar design. They both have three angular holes on a single plane, there is a supporting buttress and the outer part is angular, the ears. However it is the slight difference to the shape of the eyes (holes) that can be used as an indicator as to which country in the Mediterranean the bell was cast. This together with the quality of the bell metal, easily compared these days with a surface spectrometer, will soon give archaeologists a better idea of which foundry made the bell. The top of the *Bronze Bell* canon (left) is pointed. The Spanish Bell (right) was discovered in 2015. It is from the *San Jose* wreck, a Spanish-built galleon belonging to Philip V and sunk by the British in 1708. The eyes have a different shape and the top is flat not pointed. It also shows severe corrosion a feature of many 17th Century Spanish bells. Spanish anchors were also poorly made and show severe corrosion on similar dated wreck sites. Having similar canon rings indicates that they had wooden yokes and were hung in the same manner on both ships. This is expected as ship belfry design changed little in the 17th and early 18th centuries.

Bronze Bell

30 cm diameter
38 cm high

Photo © Paul Kay

Despite the fact that the bell has no ship's name on it, it
nevertheless provides many clues as to where the ship was built.
Because the quality of the Bronze Bell is so good it suggests it
was made in a foundry with skilled and experienced bell makers.
Bell making is a complicated process and getting everything
correct to cast a good bell demands knowledge and experience.
Stagno, Croatia had a foundry with experienced bell casters The
raw materials came from Ruskberg, western Romania, where
silver, lead, copper and iron ore was mined. As I had a notion it
was built in Croatia, I contacted the museum directors who look
after the Tower Foundry Museum in Dubrovnik, Croatia. This
particular Tower Foundry was destroyed in 1667 and would not
have been casting bells in 1677. One of my questions was, do any
of the markings on the bell relate to a small foundry at Stagno on
an island further up the coast? I failed to get a definitive answer
on this but they did confirm that the mark is the IHS stamp,
ubiquitous to Catholic bells of the time. However, I think this
mark is both the IHS and a Stagno foundry mark.

The Bronze Bell

The bell was one of the first items recovered from the site. It stands 38 cm high and has a date 1677 and the words "LAUDATE DOMINUS OMNES GENTE" (All peoples praise the Lord). The majority of European bells of this date have similar Latin lettering. It is the moulding on the bell rather than the Latin that suggests a strong Catholic bias, which could mean a source of Italy, France or Spain.

There are two moulding on the bell with a similar surround. Others have suggested they are Christ and the Virgin Mother. Although one relief does look like Mary the Virgin, I believe the other is not Christ but a picture of Leopold 1. This profile picture is similar to Leopold 1 on coins of the time. His head is always shown with a Crown of Olives, like a Roman Emperor which was his title. A picture of Christ's head is more likely depicted with a halo or a Crown of Thorns. Leopold 1 was King of Croatia and Archduke of Austria when the bell was cast in 1677. This prompted me to research Ragusa (Dubrovnik) as the place where the bell could have been cast. I surmise that the vessel was built on the Croatian shore but some of her bronze and brass fittings, including the bell may have come from Italy. The ship may have had Genoese owners from the time of its building. Bell foundry was at its peak in Europe around 1700, an estimated 60 foundries in UK alone. Bells would be made for both churches and ships, there being little difference in the design for each. Thus archaeologists sometimes think that bells found on wreck sites must be a cargo going to an ecclesiastical site and do not consider them to be the ship's bell. The position of discovery is a key as to if it is a cargo bell or not. As single bells are often found on top or to the side of wreck mounds these are likely to be the ship's bell and not part of a cargo, which would be covered in debris. For further information seek out my two e-books on Google regarding *"Bells from Shipwrecks"*.

Detail on the Bronze Bell, showing the head of Prince Leopold and the I.H.S stamp. Photograph © Paul Klay.

Bronze Bell Wreck   TOM BENNETT

Leopold 1 was King of Croatia and Archduke of Austria
Reign: 2 April 1657 – 5 May 1705   Austria from 1655 to 1705
The Bronze Bell itself has a face profile of the King of Croatia. The
head is the same as that on a Hungarian coin. It is a similar face profile,
flowing locks, and olive branch crown. There is a peculiar lump under
the nose shown on each. It is said because of inbreeding in the
Habsberg dynasty he had a large protruding jaw shown on this 1670
coin a 3 Kruezar piece. His head was also on the later Hungarian

Thaler. The Bronze Bell was
cast ten years into King
Leopold's reign and he actually
died the year the ship was
wrecked in 1709. This profile of
Leopold 1 cast into the bell, is
further evidence that the bell and
the ship were both built in
Croatia.

**Leopold I profile seen on the
Bronze Bell.** Photograph by Paul
Kay.

Minted coin used in Croatia 1670

This photograph in detail shows the symbol IHS, an abbreviation for "Jesus". In Latin speaking Christianity in medieval times it was the most common Christogram and uses the first three letters of Iesus in the Greek letters, iota-eta-sigma. When the bell was cast in 1677 it endorses the predominant Catholic faith in Ragusa, France and Italy at the time.

There was a foundry at Ston (Stagno) in Ragusa kingdom in 1677. (42 50' N 17 42' E) It was common in those days for stamps and emblems to incorporate symbolism and letters into pictures, a bit of a brain teaser, like a newspaper cartoon. The image appears to be a picture of a man standing behind the moulding of a cannon that is supported on two tresses that form a letter H. The predominant letter is S shaped like a tube, perhaps a blower to blow fumes away from the man when he pours molten bronze into the cast. A tube may also be used to suck clay dust or wood dust away from the craftsman as he makes the mould. There is a vertical line on the left of the symbol and the letters make up I H S. The main foundry in Ragusa, (Dubrovnik) was demolished in a great earthquake in 1667. It ceased functioning from this date. Many foundry workers were thought to be killed in the earthquake. Those that survived were forced to seek work elsewhere. I believe they relocated to the island of Stagno some 28 miles to the North West. I have a hunch that the Bronze Bell was made at this foundry and also some of its guns. The Medieval Foundry in the Tower at Dubrovnik is today one of the city's museum attractions and was excavated in 2009. If the bell was made in Dubrovnik itself it would display the letters SB on it, which this bell does not have.

Another Christogram seen on the Bell. "Mary the Virgin"

As a general rule ships bells after 1680 do not show the Jesuit and Catholic symbols so common before that date. Catholicism, was still strong in France and Spain, ships bells made there may retain Christian symbols until about 1730. As far as ship's bells are concerned from 1730 most Latin and Roman numerals disappear from the moulding below the neck of the bell. Many of the early ships bells, like their Church cousins, display the date it was cast and often the bell maker. FECIT before a date, is sometimes written. Later ships bells may have a ship's name cast into the bell with the date the ship was launched. After about 1830 it was common for bells to have the launch date chiselled into a body of the bell, usually below the ship's name and above the port of registry. The port name, if given, is always the port of registry and not the place where the ship was built.

From 1560 and 1570 there had been a great shipbuilding cooperation between Dubrovnik and Peschici, (41°57′0″N 16°1′0″E) which probably continued for a century. I surmise that if the bell was not made at Stagno it could well have been made at the larger bell foundry in Peschici, Italy, 155 miles across the Adriatic Sea on the opposite coastline. Perhaps the bell was designed in Croatia but cast in Italy.

Peschici Foggia, had a big shipbuilding trade and in 1572 a large ship about 750 tons was launched. Dubrovnik not to be outdone built a similar ship in 1580, a merchantman of 750 tons. These would have been the largest vessels built up to that time in Europe. It was 1630 before a Man of War was built of this size in Rotterdam. First Rate Naval ships were being built in excess of 1200 tons by the mid 17th Century. Nevertheless the Bronze Bell Ship was regarded as a very large merchant ship when built in 1677.

When she was seen aground off the beach in Dyffryn Ardudwy in 1709, the local inhabitants had never before seen such a huge ship. The shock would be akin to us seeing a Jumbo Jet arriving in our back garden!

In one of Tony Iles articles he hints at the possibility of the Vaughans trying to keep the whole thing secret, which is why we see nothing in the State Papers. There may be an element of this but on the other hand he is the local representative of the Crown and if he did everything by the book, the Privy Council may not need to be involved.

There was an assumption that Lords of the Manor could rightly claim all wreck landing on their shores. This actually only applied if the King had granted this right to them way back in the 14th Century. Only a few shorelines did this apply to, and The Gower was one. Throughout the 18th and 19th Century when Manor agreements were made, it was important that the right of wreck was included in any tenancy agreement. The windfall of a wreck and its cargo was often far in excess of any agricultural income during any one year.

However even if they had a right to the wreck landing on their foreshore, after about 1780, it was necessary for a levy of 10% to be forwarded to the Crown. From items salvaged the Customs men would decide what payment should be sent to the State Treasury. Lords of the Manor, and certainly the Vaughans managed these Port Comptrollers or King's men.

However one way of legally avoiding this 10% levy was for the Lord of the Manor to purchase the wreck from a surviving captain. If he could obtain a written purchase agreement, even for one guinea, of the entire vessel and its cargo, then the Lord of the Manor could legally do whatever he pleases with the wreck.

There is the possibility that Vaughan did just this. He thus avoided all complications of having to deal with the King's men, which probably came under his control anyway. A Genoese vessel would certainly have been insured. In order that the insurers would pay up for the losses, part of the deal to the Captain was that Vaughan would testify that the ship had been lost in deep water in the Irish Sea, lost with its entire cargo. Vaughan may have offered to transport survivors to Dublin in exchange for the entire wreck.

If Vaughan managed all these arrangements then there was no need for him to inform other authorities, hence this may the prime reason that there is an ominous silence about the wrecking.

I have seen a similar thing in the wrecking of a Dutch ship off Mumbles in 1647. The Lord of the Manor salvaged armaments and there is little mention of the event in the news of the day. *(Reference: The Silver Dollars of Rhossili, Wales, by Tom Bennett 2016)*

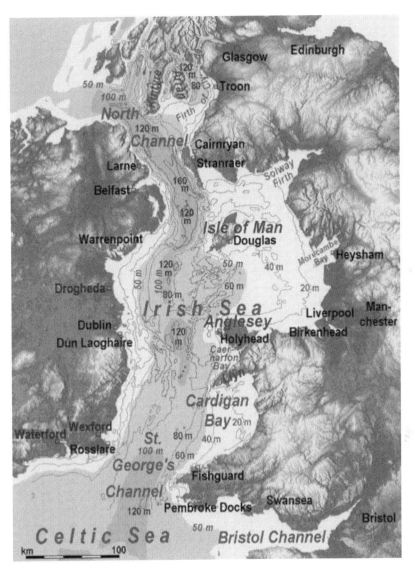

This is both a relief map and a chart (a chart is a map with depth soundings) showing position of Dublin and Cardigan Bay. It takes less than 30 hours to sail from Barmouth to Dublin. It is normally a beam reach both ways, the fastest point of sailing, thus a simple trip for Barmouth sloops.

Photograph of Bronze Bell showing the Date of 1677. As the Bell date is 32 years before the accepted date of sinking, it was conjectured that it was part of a cargo and was not the ship's bell. However, well built ships can easily last for over 60 years of age. Invariably it is the ship's bell that is found. Cargo bells would not be discovered as they would normally below a cargo mound.
Ship's bells are often the first recognisable object seen by divers, as was the case with this wreck.
In 1700 ships only carried one bell, from 1850 they carried two.

Some indicators as to why the Bronze Bell Ship could be built at Ragusa, (Dubrovnik) Croatia.

Design of the bell, Monarch's head on the bell.
Catholic influence of artefacts.
Large number of cannon
Very large merchant vessel,
Longevity of vessel
Many merchant vessels used around 1700 were Ragusan
Genoa merchants would own and charter Ragusan built vessels.
Best value for money from 1630 to 1680.
A neutral Republic during French /British war
Shape of the anchors are not French or Spanish.

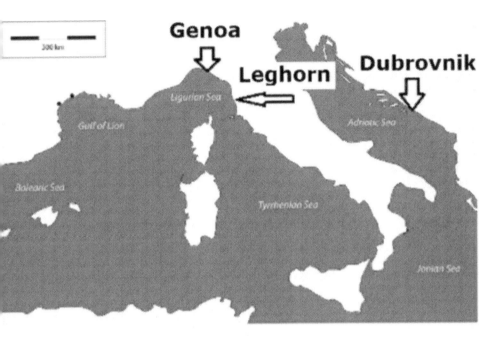

Map to show the location of Genoa and Leghorn (Livorno),in Italy.

In 1709 Genoa and Leghorn were both within the independent Republic of Genoa, Italy was a separate State. Because of symbols on the bell the author believes the ship was actually made in The Republic of Ragusa. Dubrovnik, formerly Ragusa, is in Croatia. Britain was at war with France, but both these Republics were neutral states in the year of the Bronze Bell ship was wrecked.

Slave trade in the Republic of Dubrovnik was forbidden in 1418, that is four centuries earlier than throughout the British Empire in 1833. As they did not approve of the Slave Trade their economy in the 17th and 18th Century did not benefit from the enormous profits, like America, France and Britain did.

Ragusan shipbuilding.

Before 1600, the Portuguese were regarded as the best shipbuilders, English and Ragusan vessels were a close second. By 1620 the supply of oak trees throughout Europe, needed for ship construction, was getting in short supply. The oak forests of the Portuguese Monte Gargano, also known as Monte Sant 'Angelo, had helped Portugal with this enviable claim. The Spanish relied on the oaks and pines of the Catalan Pyrenees, to build their galleys. As timber became short the Tuscany forests were needed to supply Mediterranean ship materials. Ragusan being a neutral kingdom was in a prime geographical position and economically and politically took advantage of her reputation as builders of fine ships. From 1620 onwards, Ragusa (Croatia) took over as the number one shipbuilding area, producing the best quality and largest ships in the Mediterranean. The caramusalis, light marauding vessels used by the Greeks and Turks, were built out of plane trees. The forests near Dubrovnik still had a variety of suitable timber. Galleons (merchant ships) which were expected to have a long life, required a range of woods for different parts of the ship; oak, pine, larch, ash, fir, beech and walnut. Galleys, sleeker and smaller ships, using both sail and oar power, were still in vogue, especially in the pirate trade as they could escape to windward. Oars were traditionally made in France near Marseilles and shipped to Ragusa. All other timbers used in the shipbuilding were from the local Croatian mountains.

Dubrovnik's 1395 Insurance Law is the oldest in Europe. It had all aspects of contemporary maritime insurance. Surprisingly this law is three centuries older than Lloyd's insurance, London, which dates from the end of 17th Century, which many regard as the forerunner of modern maritime insurance. Their ships carried special bombardiers, to man the guns. These could be German, French or Italian, and were not necessarily the same nationality as the ship's crew. If the British Government was a war with France they would not be agreeing to French military men being on board a chartered vessel going to Ireland.

General Hostilities in Europe. Ragusa independence

The hostilities between the Ottoman Empire and the Holy League (1683-99) were resolved in 1699 by the signing of the Treaty of Karlovci (Carlowitz), which contributed to the settlement of a number of controversial international issues. These newly-created conditions in Western Europe, were known as the Spanish War of Succession (1701-1714)` Both the small Republic of Ragusa and the Republic of Genoa had to balance themselves between opposing powers. In the case of Genoa they had France and the Kingdom of Naples as neighbours and Austria as well. It was a delicate position to maintain neutrality, and often imperilled both Republics. The Republic of Ragusa (Dubrovnik) liked to think of itself as a neutral country not showing its allegiance to either Austria or to Spain. Between 1701 and 1710 it had many diplomatic instances having to appease both warring factions. Sometimes the French would capture their ships and threatened to bombard the port when they considered Dubrovnik was erring on the side of the Austrians. This is what actually happened to Naples, when France thought that Naples allegiances fell elsewhere. The Ragusan government tolerated such an act nominally, but considered that the Republic had to be excepted of such a rule, being an inseparable part of Spanish and Austrian spheres. The senators forwarded letters to their agents in Naples and Vienna with detailed instructions of how to secure these privileges.

Persistent demands resulted in a satisfactorily conclusion. They were granted authentic documents by Emperor Joseph I himself, who recommended the protection of Ragusan interests at Naples. This confirmed loyalty and lasting devotion of the Republic to the Habsburgs, Spain and Naples. These were later endorsed in Barcelona on 22nd September 1709.

The notation on the Morris chart tells us that the Bronze Bell Ship was from Genoa or owned by Genoese merchants, or both. In the late 17th century when the ship was built the majority of large cargo ships were owned by the Dutch, Venetian or Genoese merchants. Many of these were built in the Republic of Ragusa. The quality of Ragusan ships is not disputed as there are many references. Contemporaneous Italian observers refer to the excellent craftsmanship and superior quality of Ragusan-built ships: Bartolomeo Crescenti (Rome 1602) states the best craftsmen and shipbuilders of the Mediterranean are those of Ragusa. Pantera (Rome, 1614) considers the best shipbuilders those of Ragusa, Portugal and England. Sagri (Venice 1574) contends Ragusan ships are the strongest in the world, and of the best wooden materials.

http://www.hnb.hr/dub-konf/18-konferencija/havrylyshyn-srzentic.pdf.

These references to strength and best wooden materials has a relevance to the age of the Bronze Bell Ship when it was wrecked. Some early researchers suggested that the date of 1709 and the date on the bell, 32 years before did not match up. Thus it was even thought it may not be the ship's bell but a cargo bell intended for a church.

Although ships were still being built and repaired in Genoa, Ragusa had the timber and an enviable shipbuilding industry. Their ships not only were some of the best built in the whole of Europe but they were likely to be the cheapest as well. Genoese merchants and their Jewish bankers were smart enough to get better and bigger vessels from Ragusa for the same money. This is endorsed by the fact that Oliver Cromwell had control of the British Navy and yet he commissioned at least two ships to be built in the Republic of Ragusa *Reference Roucek, in Kerner (ed.), Yugoslavia, p.136; Adamic, Native's Return, p. 152.* .These transport ships could be built without anyone else knowing about it and more convenient than getting them made in the UK or the Baltic. I have failed to find the names of any British naval ships made in Croatia, such would make interesting comparisons to the Bronze Bell Ship.

Is our Bronze Bell, one of the earliest ship's bell found?

No, the **Mary Rose** bell is 167 years older and a ship's bell has been found on a Venetian shipwreck with 1527 date on it. Off the Oman coast is an early Portuguese East Indian trader wreck sunk in 1503 with a bell dated 1489. The earliest bell found on a wreck site is in Finland. Considered by the present custodians to be a church bell but I believe it to be a ship's bell. It is dated to about 1330 and thought to be cast in Belgium.

The **Mary Rose** bell found at the stern of the ship is one of the earliest ship's bells found in UK waters. The bell is cast in bronze. It has a total height of 221 mm, including the suspension loop and an external dimension of 208 mm at the mouth. It weighs just over 5 kilos. The average thickness of the metal is 15 mm. The ship's name **Mary Rose** was not found on the bell, while the only markings were from the maker and the casting date. An inscription around the top in Lombardic script in Flemish reads "I was made in 1510". It is believed the bell was made in Antwerp, Belgium. Of significance is that the holding piece at the top of the crown has a simple ring as in modern ships bells. With our present knowledge of ship's bells and anchors from known shipwrecks it should now be possible to formulate a meaningful typology software application to aid historians in dating and identifying unidentified shipwrecks, using dimensions and photographs of known bells and dated anchors. Once an estimated date and size of the vessel is calculated, cross references to ship losses in that particular area on indexes can determine likely candidates. That is why all shipwreck databases need to be as accurate as possible. Unfortunately, Coflein at the moment, are not providing the required accuracy in their Welsh shipwreck database.

One of the earliest recorded mention of the ship's bell was on the British ship *Grace Dieu* launched 1514. She was twice the size of the Bronze Bell ship and her wreck site still remains in the Hamble. No bigger ship was built in England for another 200 years.

Other artefacts found on the Bronze Bell Wrecksite include a gunner's rule, buttons, lead shot and cannon balls.

A swivel gun, extracted from the wreck site under licence and conserved by the Royal Armouries. Part of the display at Ty Gwyn. Photograph © MADU.

At least two of the cannon were loaded which indicates that they were in active use and not being used as extra ballast on the ship.

Below is a display at Ty Gwyn of cannon balls and bar shot. The latter was not to fire at the hull but to fire into the rigging to tear sails and sever shrouds.

Photograph©Chris Holden

Display of cannon balls and bar-shot seen at the Ty Gwyn Museum . Chain-shot and Bar-shot; two iron balls joined together with a chain or bar. This type of shot was particularly effective against rigging, boarding netting, and sails. Once the sails were disabled the ship could be captured while it was still floating. The value for pirates and corsairs was both the ship and the cargo. They did not want to sink their prey as they would lose both. A captured merchant ship could be towed or have a new crew put on board to re-rig her and sail her away with the cargo still intact.

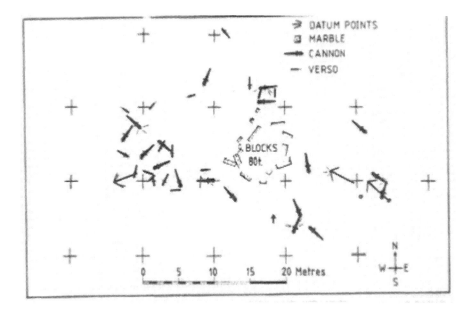

Plan of site showing position of the cannon, swivel guns and anchors. As most of the armaments are on the west side that would be stern of the ship. Two anchors are at the bow but these would be secondary anchors not the large bower anchors which are missing altogether, assume salvaged rather than deployed. If the ship hit the reef and was wrecked in the same direction as it was travelling, it suggests that the captain was sailing northwards close to the beach at the time. On the site plan the mound of marble blocks are seen to be in the centre of the wreck site. The bell was found in an area to the West of the marble blocks, i.e., more aft of amidships. When the **The Mary Rose** bell was found, that too was in the aft section of the ship and this is where a single belfry was traditionally placed. The bell, was housed in a large wooden (sometimes walnut) belfry and regarded as the 'altar piece' on board the vessel. Wrecks discovered in the last ten years in cold Baltic water from a similar age show these structures in their entirety.

Bronze Bell Wreck   TOM BENNETT

Diagram to show how to date a pewter platter. Using this diagram the six platters found at the wreck site fall into the date category of 1640 to 1680.

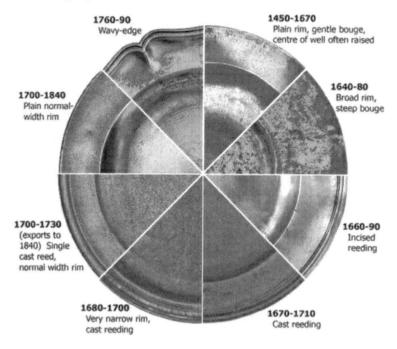

1760-90
Wavy-edge

1450-1670
Plain rim, gentle bouge,
centre of well often raised

1640-80
Broad rim,
steep bouge

1700-1840
Plain normal-
width rim

1660-90
Incised
reeding

1700-1730
(exports to
1840) Single
cast reed,
normal width rim

1680-1700
Very narrow rim,
cast reeding

1670-1710
Cast reeding

Finding any pewter plates on a wreck site without associated pottery plates instantly dates the wreck to before 1730. Wreck sites after 1747 show more pottery pieces. As the site has not been thoroughly excavated there could be more platters and personal items yet to be discovered.

The Captain and officers were usually from rich families and, like their upbringing, would have had silverware and silver platters. It is said that much silverware found its way into Cors Y Gedol Mansion, (no reference). Wooden platters may also have been used, but the observed wreck site is devoid of almost all wood artefacts and timbers.

Founder members of the Cae Nest Group, the late Mike Bower (left) and Tony Iles (right) with three of the six pewter platters recovered from the site. One of these platters is shaped like a cardinal's hat with a hallmark stamp of Lyon dated 1700. Obviously made in France this

was one reason why early investigation suggested the ship was also of French origin. A Croatian crew member could have acquired it on his travels or swapped it for one marked Rome! Lyon is up the River Rhone from Marseilles and we know that there was a lot of trade and movement of people between Genoa and this French port. It probably belonged to a soldier or sailor that had been on the ship during its trading over 32 years. The ship would have traded with the port of Marseilles on numerous occasions. A stack of four pewter plates were found on the wreck site. They were concreted to an iron cannon. Sid Wignall suggested that the site may have been covered in sand at one time causing this to happen. It is unlikely that there still remains a great number of platters still on the seabed.

Bronze Bell Wreck   TOM BENNETT

Pewter platters in the Ty Gwyn Museum. Photo; © Chris Holden

One silver fork has been recovered from the wreck, others may have found their way to the Manor. Silverware was only used by the Captain and his officers, and a single fork suggests it had found its way into the bilges of the ship before it was wrecked. These often show the family crest or name of the ship. Silverware and pewter items at Cors y Gedol may give us more clues as to the Genoese ownership of the Bronze Bell Ship.

Evidence from the **Mary Rose** on wooden plates and pewter ware suggest that tankards and plates were the individual's property. Other artefacts found included a gunner's rule, buttons, and coins. The gunner's rule is in much better condition than the one recovered from the **Mary Rose**, and may be the best example yet recovered from a wreck site of this date. However over the last few years some early 18th Century wrecks have been discovered in the cold Baltic water with timbers and bronze showing virtually no corrosion or deterioration. When their artefacts are recovered our knowledge of 17th and 18th Century ships will be enhanced in leaps and bounds.

A cannon ball found in the garden of Cors y Gedol is known to fit one of the Bronze Bell cannons. However, I am not surprised as the cannon found on the wreck are of a range of sizes and similar to land cannon of the day.

Bronze Bell Wreck   TOM BENNETT

Gunner's Rule

Photograph:© Alan Vincent 2017.

A 10 inch brass rule with a figurine handle. Searching on the Internet a gunner's rule seemed to be a pair of dividers or calipers and often confused with a clinometer. I now see that they were calipers to measure the diameter of the cannon ball, to calculate the charge needed to fire it efficiently. The ruler rod discovered on the Bronze Bell site has marks and numerals from 0 to 100. It is a far simpler instrument but does the same thing. I am told that the scale on each side of the rule is different. It has been suggested that one side may relate to iron cannon balls and the other to lead cannon balls. However it may also differentiate Chain shot as opposed to a solid cannon ball.

The Specific Gravity of lead is 11.35, Iron shot 3.15 and Stone shot 2.4 -2.7

We now have to ask ourselves, was this object used by the gunners of the swivel guns or by the larger iron cannon, or both?

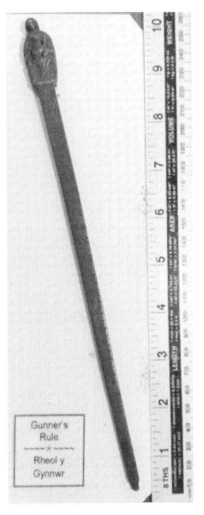

Gunner's Rule
~~~~✕~~~~
Rheol y Gynnwr

The figure on the Gunner's Rule was obviously going to be a patron saint of gunners. Originally I thought this was the patron saint of bombardiers, Saint Quintinus, a Roman who was killed in France in the 3rd Century. He is sometimes depicted seated and with a sword. I then realized there is a much more important martyr related to gunners. This 'sword' is a palm frond being held by Saint Barbara. The telling feature is the two smaller figures on her right side. It is showing her father standing holding her head by her hair after decapitating her with his sword. Thus it is definitely Saint Barbara an early Christian Greek martyr. Today Saint Barbara is known throughout the military as the patron saint of artillerymen, and her image was at one time placed frequently on arsenals and powder magazines. The powder storage room of a French warship is still called Sainte-Barbe and in Venice their *Scuola dei Bombardiera* was dedicated to her.

Photograph: © Alan Vincent 2017

I was hoping that one scale on the gunners rule was intended for stone-made cannon balls, suggesting it related to the earlier swivel guns. Hand made stone shot faded out during the 17th Century. The swivel guns were actually found loaded with lead shot. The gunners rule could still be one of the few items relating to an earlier vessel on the site.

Bronze Bell Wreck   TOM BENNETT

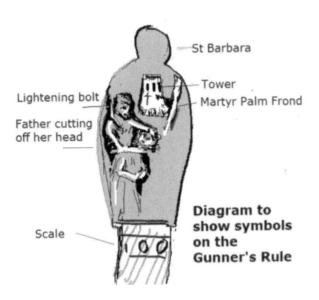

Lightening bolt

Father cutting
off her head

St Barbara

Tower

Martyr Palm Frond

Scale

**Diagram to
show symbols
on the
Gunner's Rule**

The story of Saint Barbara is varied. Basically she was a repressed young lady in Izmit, Turkey in the 3rd Century. Her widowed rich grain dealer father locked her away in a tower, so that she would not be influenced by the outside world. However as she grew up she became a devote Christian. At last her father considered her mind had been affected by her seclusion so he let her have her freedom. While he was away a bathhouse was being built at their home. Instead of the two window design Barbara got the workmen to put in three windows like a Holy Trilogy. Her furious father reported her faith to the Roman authorities and she was condemned to death for her beliefs. After being tortured and humiliated in public she would not give up her faith or agree to marriage. Her father was given the task of her execution. Soon after her beheading, he was struck down with a thunderbolt of lightning and was killed. In the 7th Century some four centuries after her death she became venerated by those who wanted protection from sudden explosion, fire and lightning. She was adopted as the patron saint of artillery men and those in the mining industry. Even today she is the patron saint of the Italian Navy.

Bronze Bell Wreck   TOM BENNETT

Other artefacts found on the site include navigation dividers, fine cutlery, a dental plate and remains of pistols, a rapier and hilts of other swords. Coins representing ten different countries have been found on or near the wreck site, further enhancing the notion that the ship or members of its complement had travelled extensively throughout the European region.

The author has had some difficulty in estimating the number of crew and soldiers carried on board the ship. British Naval ships carrying 40 guns may have in excess of 150 men on board. Merchant ships even today are not allowed to train and arm their crew. However they are allowed to carry mercenary soldiers who can protect the crew, cargo and the ship. This is what has been happening over the last 15 years to protect merchant ship from Somali and Nigerian pirates. Thus the numbers of people on board the Bronze Bell Ship are composed of two distinct groups one being the Ship's crew and the other being the militia. The numbers of soldiers and bombardiers would have been at least 50 men, this number only sufficient to man ten cannon at any one time, with ten soldiers spare to use small arms. As for the number of ordinary sailors we have to consider the activities undertaken and the number of watches (rotation of crew, giving some time for sleep). Bower anchors would require a large capstan (horizontal man powered deck winch) to lift them. Large ships required 32 men, to move the capstan arms in order to lift one anchor. At the same time there would be similar number of men hauling up and trimming sails in the act of sailing away when the anchor was lifted. This adds up to 64 men in the crew, 50 military and 6 officers; some 130 men. I would guess that the crew and the soldiers each had their own pewter platter. 130 platters have not been seen on the wreck site, indicating that these personal possessions were carried off the wreck in an unhurried fashion. The lack of hundreds of small arms similarly gives the same supposition. The soldiers on board, if they disembarked in an orderly manner could have taken their possessions (pewter plates?), small arms and rapiers with them.

Flag of the Dutch West Indian Company as seen flying on this well-armed Dutch ship.

Thought to be the **Princess** wrecked at Swansea in 1647

This is a similar, large, heavily-armed Dutch merchant ship. She flies the flag of the Dutch West India Company. Although this ship looks very similar to the ship in the Leghorn painting of 1700; it cannot be as the **Princess** was wrecked in 1647 near Swansea, South Wales. The **Princess** carried 111 people including ten passengers. When she broke up fast on Mumbles Point no less than 80 persons drowned. I would guess the total number (crew plus soldiers) carried by the Bronze Bell Ship would be 130 people. I have failed to find any record of a mass burial happening near Harlech in 1709 so the author assumes the wreck did not break up quickly and there was an orderly abandonment of those on board.

My theory that the wreck lay intact for a week before breaking up is based on lack of burials, lack of personal articles, artefacts at Cors y Gedol, small number of marble blocks seen and the number of anchors that remain on the wreck site . There was an opportunity to remove valuable swivel guns and other cannon if the wreck lay intact for days before she broke up, but this was not done. The Captain may have still considered that she could be floated off and repaired. It was up to the Captain to say what should be taken off the ship and in what order. If the wreck lay semi derelict for ten days, and was obviously not going to sail again, Vaughan himself may have struck a deal with the Captain. He may have offered to transport all the crew and soldiers to Dublin, in exchange for the wrecked ship and all its cannon. The Captain, who probably was not a Welsh speaker, was in no position to bargain as he had to go through Vaughan, the King's representative, to organise anything. Vaughan would have his own trading sloops, based in Barmouth, that regularly traded over to Dublin. The cost of doing a few trips across the Irish Sea, to take salvaged cargo and the survivors, was to Vaughan was a trifling sum. Vaughan knew that the timbers, masts, fitments and iron that could be salvaged was of immeasurable value. Furthermore Vaughan, as owner of the wreck, would not be liable to pay to the Crown the 10% that otherwise he was obliged to do. I believe some marble and paper went to Dublin. I am also of the opinion that the survivors also left Wales via Dublin. This scenario fits in well with the fact that many of the timbers from the ship were used two years later in the construction of buildings at Cors y Gedol. It may also be the reason why marble blocks and guns were not recovered by divers once the ship was wrecked. Vaughan was already rich and after he had acquired as much building timber as he needed, he never organised any diving operations at the wreck site. Local fishermen were warned off the site as they knew it belonged to the Lord of the Manor.

Local fishermen would not have the expertise to lift the remaining marble or cannon and not have the money to employ a diver, who would probably have to come from Cornwall. Nobody would be in a position to organise salvage of the wreck without prior permission of Vaughan, whether or not he had purchased the hulk from the Captain. Private salvers would not want the complications of dealing with the High Sheriff. As the proximity of Cors y Gedol was so close and in sight of the wreck, it would been impossible to salvage without him knowing about it. Thus the wreck site remained untouched.

State paper mentions the Duke of Marlborough in June 1709 suggests to his wife by letter that one marble statue block, already in London, is used to fit out the buffet room in Marlborough House. This Pall Mall residence was being completed in 1711. I have yet to find which marble block he is referring to, but with a bit of imagination it could be one salvaged from Talybont.

Measuring a marble block at the site for the original survey in 1979. Photo: © Tony Iles.

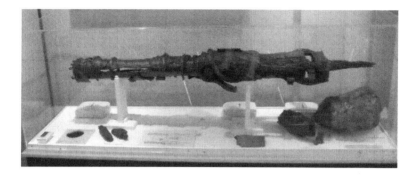

A display at Ty Gwyn Museum showing one of the four swivel guns that have been conserved. Photograph; © Chris Holden.

The number of cannon found on the Bronze Bell wreck site is at least 32. Six of which are a set of swivel guns from the 15th Century.

If we are seeking a painting of a ship that looked like the Bronze bell Ship we are looking for a large ship with at least 16 gun ports on each side of the hull. Having found that the State of Genoa had a 34 gun Frigate that was sold of at the end of the 17th Century, somewhat complicates the story. However this ship could have been sold off to be chartered as a privateer or merchantman. Thus a large naval looking ship that could also carry some cargo. If this ship is our Bronze Bell Ship then it is likely to be manned entirely by sailors and soldiers from Genoa. In those days, captains of large ships, usually stayed with their ships for their entire lives. He would know the vessel he commanded inside out. He was accustomed to manage and navigate her, understanding her sail speeds and idiosyncrasies. The captain of this ship was not expected to negotiate selling the cargos. When merchandise was taken, some of the prime merchants would also accompany the voyage. These merchants always marked their goods to distinguish which was theirs.

This brass figurine is one of the most intriguing artefacts from the Bronze Bell Wreck. It is a tactile object designed to be held in the hand to stamp a large and a small seal. The figure depicts a musician with a bagpipe. He has a large beard and holds aloft a bell that is the smaller seal. The opening between his legs is to allow a finger or thumb to be inserted to give additional downward pressure when applying the stamp.

The left hand of the figure holds a bagpipe but as the pipe has a decided curve in it is also made to look like the man is masturbating an oversize penis. Altogether it is a humorous piece and makes the payment of taxes or the purchase of goods more bearable.

The seal found may be a seal to identify the paper company. Paper may have come from ten different suppliers and each would want mark their goods with a seal. Perhaps this is why it has a small and a large seal, to mark different sizes of paper.

This is an early photograph of a elderly musician and his young accomplice, thought to be on the streets of Genoa. He holds a stick to hit annoying dogs and has a bagpipe. His beard and hat are the same as the man in the hand seal.

A Habsberg seal from the wreck site, considered to be a Berath Seal. Used by an agent to confirm that a tax has been made for Muslim goods travelling into Europe. It is not known whether the above seal and the hand seal were made for each other, or if it is another seal found nearby. At the top of the crest is the Austrian Eagle. Surrounding letters are PPGC. These may be the initials of the Berath or shipping agent.

Beraths, Berats and Seals.
At the beginning of the eighteenth century we see the plurality of legal contracts, one being the legal contract of Europeans (non Muslims) and the other via Beraths, a legal format whereby Muslims can trade with their European partners. This was increasingly important for the Levant and Ottoman trade. If Muslims wanted to trade in Europe they needed to purchase beraths or have agents to supply such. All Muslim trade from Syria, Turkey to Albania was done through such contracts. One of the cargos from Leghorn at the time was silk which would have meant Muslim trade and a berat agreement. The berath provided tax privileges and reduced rates for Muslims on the various taxes being enforced.

Yanni Mavrogordota was a beratlı of Sweden. He operated with two beratlı partners in Izmir and merchant houses in Izmir, Chios and Amsterdam. These partners did "a quarter of trade of Holland in the quality of commissioners and a lot of business in other places of Italy." Gio Mavrogordato and Gio Anastasio were beratlı partners. They had a firm Gio Mavrogordato, Gio Anatasi and Company. They in turn did business with a Petri Petrocokino and Catansino, a partnership of two Swedish beraths. They had signed consignments to the Dutch merchant De Bok for their merchandize in Amsterdam.

The Habsberg seal found has the letters PPGC. I was conjecturing that these may be the letters of Petri Petrocokino (Gio ?) Catansino. They in the eighteenth century were shipping agents for Dutch goods coming out of Smyrna and destined for Amsterdam. Ships with a marble cargo out from Leghorn at this time also carried silk. Silk arriving in Levant, Smyrna or Leghorn would have come overland via the Silk Road route from China. To trade silk in the West from Muslin Turkey, Albania and Syria required the use of a Berath. The Ambassadors of each country were allowed to sell or auction up to about 30 Berats to the Berath agents. This provided a considerable income for the ambassadors. The Levant Company in 1706 tried to stop the practice and form a more free trade. They were not very successful and the berath system continued.

If the PPGC seal has been identified correctly, there is now a suggestion that our Bronze Bell ship may have previously traded to Amsterdam, perhaps taking marble and silks to that Dutch city. Marble to build the Royal Chapel at Versailles was sometimes routed in Dutch and Genoese ships to Amsterdam. This fact brings to mind another curious supposition. The Bronze Bell Ship may have been no stranger to sailing in the English Channel. Ten years previously she could have been transporting marble and silks to Amsterdam, with the marble ending up in the Palace of Versailles. Other cargoes that came from Leghorn included Tuberose Roots and wine. The roots are the heavily scented flower (Polianthes tuberosa) On February 4th 1709 the London Gazette advertised "There is lately brought from Leghorn a parcel of choice Tuberose Roots which are to be sold at the King's Head, London." I wonder if the Bronze Bell Ship also carried some plants which ended up in Cors y Gedol gardens or in the Italian garden at Blenheim Palace.

On February 13th 1709 there is news that some ships were being fitted out in Genoa. 'The Duke of Tursis is fitting out six gallies at Genoa which is supposed to be designed to transport the French Cardinals from Marseilles to Rome, that they may assist in the Election of a new Pope, in case of the decease of his present Holiness!'

This shows that both ships and crews were constantly passing between Marseilles and Genoa. The pewter platter found with Lyon hallmark could easily have been the private possession of a French soldier who had previously travelled to Genoa to join the Bronze Bell Ship as a military man. Having said this, it now seems likely that if the British Government was chartering the entire vessel and were also providing an old Man O' War to protect the vessel on her voyage to Dublin. Britain was at war with France and the Bronze Bell Ship may have changed its soldiers and bombardiers from French to Italian military, for this particular trip. Although possible, it is highly unlikely that **HMS Neptune** supplied gunners and soldiers to man the Bronze Bell Ship as that would deplete their own complement. However the **Neptune** could have delivered British military personal to Leghorn for that purpose. Although the Bronze Bell ship was on charter, I think it was not a bare-boat charter. The Captain would have been from Genoa or Croatia, would have shares in the ship and benefited from any profits. The crew would be the usual crew of the ship but the militia nationality would be arranged by the chatterer. When the ship was lost it would have been properly insured. That had always been the custom with Ragusa ships, who operated ship insurance generations before Lloyds of London.

The author cannot be certain that the Bronze Bell was escorted by
HMS Neptune . The reference talks about **Neptune** "of and for
London". The entry could have said *Her Majesty's ship Neptune.*
However it does say she was from Leghorn and does not mention any
cargo. If she had cargo the newspaper would normally describe it. The
lack of mentioning any cargo suggests she had none and was a privateer
rather than a merchant ship. When in the English Channel she captures
a French frigate. This infers the **Neptune** was a large naval vessel with
many more guns than the French Naval vessel. **HMS Neptune** was a
90-gun second rate launched in 1683. She was rebuilt in 1710 and 1730
before being renamed **HMS Torbay** in her new incarnation as a third
rate in 1750. She was sold in 1784. Thus this ship had an active life in
excess of a hundred years. If the same **Neptune** she was was 26 years
old in 1709 and would have sailed at the same speed as the Bronze Bell
Wreck.

She departed Leghorn at the same time as the Bronze Bell Ship and it
was probably providing protection against piracy for the chartered
vessel until the Bronze Bell Ship met St Georges Channel, when the
two ships left each other's company. It is difficult for two ships to sail
together, even in the best of weather. However I get the impression that
in the days before accurate charts, merchant ships commonly did so to
both help each other in navigation and be at hand if any disaster was to
befall the accompanying ship. Certainly in times of war and with piracy
rife, ship captains knew that there was always safety in numbers.

It is not clear what nationalities made up the crew of the Bronze Bell
Ship. It could even have been British sailors with Royal Navy soldiers
and gunners. Just two years before, the Royal Navy had lost 2000 of
their best men when the British fleet was wrecked on the Isles of Scilly.
In 1709 the Royal Navy were desperately short of ratings. More likely
the vessel was chartered with its own crew and usual military on board.
To show its independence the Genoese, I surmise, normally chartered
the ship with French military, but this group would have been swapped
for another nationality for this particular trip.

The time involved and the process of writing this text has enabled me to get a picture of what likely happened in 1709.

A Croatian built ship in 1677, was owned by a Genoese family. It was a huge merchant ship, still unnamed, and was heavily armed. Nationality of the crew unknown but likely to be from Genoa and Republic of Ragusa. It carried an unknown number of crew and soldiers . The soldiers could be from any nationality but likely Italian, French or Austrian.

Christopher Wren, the architect building St Paul's in London had ordered marble blocks from Genoa. During January or February 1709 this marble together with a cargo of paper was sailing to Dublin. Dublin was the destination port as the French were capturing vessels going to London, and the Catholic crew were not welcomed in England. The marble was to be loaded into another merchant ship in Dublin and forwarded, under escort of an HM Navy vessel to London. Due to a very slight error in navigation the ship found itself near Sarn Badrig on the Welsh coast. This is about 95 miles away from Dublin. In an attempt to sail landward of Sarn Badrig the ship grounded and failed to get off an underwater reef. There was no loss of life and the ship remained upright and fairly intact for a fortnight. Vaughan, the local Lord of the Manor bought the grounded ship from the Captain. Some 70% (my guess) of the marble and paper cargo was successfully salvaged before the wreck broke apart and sank. The salvaged cargo and the survivors were taken to Dublin from whence they could forward to their respective destinations. Once the wreck had broken apart and sank there was no more salvage of the marble at the site.

As Vaughan, happened to be at the scene and acted for the Crown, there was no need for letters to be sent to London about the wrecking. Hence it never was reported in the newspapers and evaded being documented in the State Papers.

During 1998, along with members of the Tewkesbury Underwater Group , **MADU** (Malvern Archaeological Diving Unit) assisted with the survey and recording of the cannons, anchors and cargo of marble blocks. This survey was enhanced in 2004 and in 2006 a full Archaeological Report was made by Wessex Archaeology, commissioned by CADW. Previous to that Sydney Wignall, one of the first Licence Holders of the site had written a report of the wreck site, in the same year as it was designated an Historic Wreck. The Wessex Archaeology report show that much thought has gone into the wrecking process. Some of the anomalies are made much clearer if there is an acceptance of my wrecking theory that the wreck did not break up quickly. For a ship to sail from Cape Finistaire to Dublin, in strong Westerly winds without sight of land for five days, could easily end up 90 miles West of its intended destination. The navigation error is only a few degrees of under-correction of leeway drift. The tonnage of marble still existing is only a fraction of the tonnage needed to ballast a ship of 700 tons. My theory being that the ship did not smash up and sink within a few hours, drowning the majority of the crew. The ship was sailing sedately and cautiously Southward of the causeway of Sarn Badrig. Her captain may have seen breaking water on the Western end of Sarn Badrig. Being over nine miles out to sea he may not have seen land to the East and so sailed in that direction. He still assumed he was off the Irish coast until trapped near the beach at Dyffryn Ardudwy. The inner shallow channel, was much used by the Porthmadoc schooners 150 years later as a route to get away from the Causeway. This channel has a reef running parallel to the beach, its position would only be known to the local captains and pilots. The Bronze Bell Ship grounded on this reef and not the main St Patrick's Causeway (Sarn Badrig). The fact that 26 cannon and three anchors still lie on the seabed, strongly suggest that no underwater salvage took place in 1709. I believe that the ship did not sink straight away but remained afloat long enough for most of the marble to be taken off.

Coins from the site and some washed up on the shoreline provide a coverage of no less than ten countries. The coins indicate that the crew or the ship had travelled extensively and may have done voyages as far as Amsterdam in its 32 years of trading. The Habsberg seal if it is a Berath seal, also indicates that the vessel may have traded with Amsterdam in the past. The most recent coin found is dated 1702.

Even if the Captain was familiar with sailing in the English Channel I am convinced that on this occasion he was taking the goods, albeit for London, to Dublin. The majority of his crew were Catholic and since the middle of the 17th Century and the Civil War, there was a prejudice against Catholics in London and at all the south of England ports. Many ships in 1708 and 1709 from Genoa and Leghorn sailed to Dublin with goods for London. Dublin had a greater empathy for Catholic crews and it was an easier port to sail to than to London. The main reason was to avoid unnecessary problems in the English Channel and the exposure of capture by French frigates and corsairs. There are other reasons for not sailing direct to London. The British Navy was so short of man power that they would prey on British vessels sailing out of London. It was common practice for them to commandeer one in five of the sailors from the merchant ships. This is why some merchant ships would sail alone, not wanting to wait for a Naval escort, knowing some of their best sailors may be taken away from them. Some merchant ships, leaving London, apprehended by HM Naval ships in 'The Downs' (off Kent coast) found themselves so short handed that they were forced to return to port to collect new crew. I can think of two more reasons not wanting to sail direct to London. One was that February was the worst month for fog in the Channel and the other that it was nearer to the German and Dutch ports which were still recovering from the Plague that was rife just forty years before.

Goods arriving in Dublin were transferred to other merchant ships that were then sailing to London. Some would wait for a Navy ship and then sail for London in a convoy with Naval protection. Sometimes ships having crossed the Atlantic would sail into Kinsale, before unloading or venturing on to London. However Dublin was a much bigger port and had more commercial links with London. As Illsley states, a three-degree compass error in setting course from Cape Finisterre to Plymouth could put a vessel in St George's Channel. Plymouth cannot be reached on a single bearing, but I know what he is trying to convey is that three degrees West of an intended way point for the English Channel. That it does not need much to go wrong to end up 90 miles away from where was intended. Only two degrees would cause a ship to be the wrong side of the Irish Sea. The London Gazette stated that there were strong Westerlies on 3rd February 1709. To seafaring men that means force 6-8, gale force winds but not a storm. As I believe the ship was half way or nearing the end of its voyage to Dublin, these Westerlies must have contributed to the Bronze Bell ship loss. Either in putting the ship into Cardigan Bay or by pounding her to bits when she was already aground. Apart from these known strong Westerlies, the cold temperature across Europe was extreme. The coastal strip surrounding Britain froze over and even the Adriatic and Mediterranean sea around the coast was frozen from Marseilles to Genoa. The Seine above Paris for three months was frozen in, no ships could get fresh food along the Seine to Versailles. The ground was frozen up to 9 feet in depth, crops, shrubs, vegetables were destroyed, wheat prices doubled. Olive trees in the South of France were decimated, the finest citrus and orange groves in Italy were destroyed. and 24000 people were meant to have died of cold and starvation in Paris alone. The death toll throughout France was about 2.5% of the population. Toulouse temperatures were one degree colder than Paris. They were sub arctic temperatures. Even Louise XIV in his luxurious palace in Versailles was feeling the cold, (serves him right for building such big rooms).

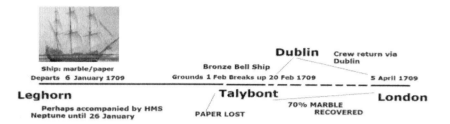

Ship: marble/paper
Departs 6 January 1709

Leghorn

Perhaps accompanied by HMS
Neptune until 26 January

Bronze Bell Ship
Grounds 1 Feb Breaks up 20 Feb 1709

Dublin   Crew return via Dublin

5 April 1709

Talybont

PAPER LOST

70% MARBLE
RECOVERED

London

I surmise the timeline would be as shown above. As soon as Vaughan heard from the Captain that there was a Government cargo aboard, he would have sent news to Dublin via a Barmouth sloop. All news had to travel via ship and that was the quickest way to inform London of what had happened. Within two days of grounding the news had reached the agent in Dublin. Within four days of grounding a Dublin vessel could be alongside the wreck helping with salvage or the dismantling of masts and rigging. This would make sense, as the Government agent was still in control. Let us assume this happened, the Dublin shipper sends a ship over to Talybont to help with salvage and secure some of the marble blocks. Some marble and paper could then be transferred directly from the wreck into a ship that could take the salvaged goods directly to London. A large ship could also take all the survivors as well. However, the survivors / crew were more likely to return home via Dublin, as it was quicker, cheaper and more Catholic friendly route. This further implies that more than one vessel would have been sent across from Dublin to Talybont. One to take the survivors to Dublin, another for cargo shipment to London and possibly another to help dismantle masts and rigging and transport those to London. The Royal Navy was always in need of masts, sails and rigging especially from such a large ship as the Bronze Bell ship. She was a size similar to the Men O' War lost two years before on the Isles of Scilly. The lack of pulleys and dead-eyes seen at the wreck site, to me suggests that the masts, shrouds and rigging were all taken away at the time of wrecking.

The London Gazette was a single sheet newspaper that was published every three day in the heart of London. I have searched closely through all news from 1st January to 1st April 1709, hoping to find something about the Bonze Bell Ship. There was news from Cowes on 4th February 1709, that the London ship **Neptune**, Roger Goodcheap, Master, inward from Leghorn had captured and brought in the 12 gun and 85 men French Privateer named **Countess of Dieppe**, which he took off Portland on Thursday last. This **Neptune** could be the **HMS Neptune** a 90 gun Man O' War that was providing protection and accompanied the Bronze Bell Ship from Leghorn to St George's Channel. The **Neptune** then departed company with the Bronze Bell when off the Isles of Scilly. Roger Goodcheap her Captain may have considered that the Bronze Bell Ship needed no more protection and could find her own way to Dublin. This would make the grounding date of the wreck about first week of February 1709.

Although Genoa was a port that repaired and built ships, there were many ship owners of that port that had their ships built in Croatia. A 700 ton vessel was massive for that period and as Croatia had the expertise and raw materials for shipbuilding, there is a strong possibility that this vessel was constructed there. The established bell foundry in Dubrovnik had been damaged in an earthquake prior to 1677 and as the bell does not have Dubrovnik 'Saint Blaise' symbol on it is unlikely to be be cast in the Ragusan capital. There is a possibility that the bell was cast in one of the two main bell foundries on the Italian shore opposite.

The bell shows strong Catholic symbolism. It also has the head of the monarch of Croatia, similar to Croatian coins of that time. Croatian ships were well constructed and were known for their longevity. The Bronze Bell Ship was 32 years old when wrecked which for a Croatian built ship was expected. Heavily and strongly constructed ships built in West Wales mid eighteenth century would often be over 42 years old when wrecked and some were still sailing when over 100 years old. (See book by Tom Bennett, Maritime History of Newport Pembrokeshire. Wales, 2017, Amazon paperback)

Further Research.
I have an idea for a suitable study for a budding Geologist or Architect
doing a degree course. Especially one interested in marble architectural
features. Using the non destructive method of Spectrometry a hand
held unit could be used to compare all the various marble features that
may be associated with the Bronze Bell Wreck. The marble block
carved by the late Frank Cocksey is known to be from the wreck site. If
the microscopic particles of its surface can be compared with other
marble features, the likelihood of them being salvaged from the wreck
site is made more certain. A comparison of the "Last Haul" marble
with floor tiles in St Paul's. Floor tiles in the middle of the long aisle at
St Paul's are Carrara marble but of a previous shipment, and hence a
different part of the quarry. These surfaces could be compared to tiles
next to or near Kilkenny black marble (black with many small crustacea
imbedded in it), thought to be laid in 1709. Black marble steps on the
west end are of Irish marble put there in 1708/9. If there are any Bronze
Bell white marble it is likely found to the side of the choir area.
Secondly the marble on the Queen's Statue outside St Paul's is the most
likely candidate to be the same marble as the "Last Haul". Thirdly the
fountain outside Blenheim Palace. One of the statues inside Blenheim
Palace may also be the same marble. It is expected that all Carrara
Marble carried in one shipment is from the same part of one quarry and
will have a similar but not identical surface. I am expectant of
microscopic differences in different parts of the same quarry and that
one shipment will be of a different quality to another. Hopefully this
will determine a meaningful comparison. Near identical surfaces
would help my theory that some of the Bronze Bell Wreck marble did
in fact get to the St Paul's site. This would also support my theory that
the some of the blocks were salvaged from the site in February or
March 1709, giving us a more accurate date of the wrecking.
It would also be helpful if someone passionate about researching
ancestral records, could look in detail at the local church records. To
both confirm that there were no burials in 1709 and to study foreign
names within the Weddings, Baptisms, and Deaths between the wreck
date (1709) and up to 60 years later.

Using high powered microscopic cameras the surfaces of two white marble pieces can be compared with some degree of accuracy.

An underwater archaeologist Beltrame wrote a paper on a marble ship discovered at Crotone, Italy. It had sculptured beading and fluting on pieces of different marbles, the quarries being determined by the microscopic surfaces of the marble pieces. This wreck was determined to be 18th Century the same as the Bronze Bell Wreck.

Detail of Carrara white marble when seen in macro and and micro-photograph of thin section (N+, 16¥) of white Carrara marble. (L. Lazzarini)

From Figure 11, of paper Beltrame : Underwater Investigation of a marble wreck. Crotone, Italy.

I am no expert on such an examination but I am convinced if tiles from near the west steps of St Paul's could be carefully compared to the "Last Haul" marble we could microscopically tell if they were from the same part of the same Tuscany quarry. Tony Iles informs me that some of the Bronze Bell blocks have a groove cut into them like a prefabricated unit. This is very similar to the Marble Wreck at Crotone, where blocks were fluted and moulded before being shipped.

White marble blocks taken from Scotland Yard in April 1709 were used to construct a fountain at Blenheim Palace, Woodstock, Oxfordshire. I am not sure which of the many fountains it was made into but I would guess it is the "Mermaid Fountain" in the Italian Garden. In the last thirty years this ornate statue has been repainted and it is difficult to tell what pieces may relate to eight pieces of white marble. This photograph shows the central mermaid painted black but I think she could be made of white Carrara marble, salvaged from the Bronze Bell wreck before it broke up. Skilled sculptors could have been amongst passengers carried on the Bronze Bell Ship. Although Christopher Wren may have had Italian marble craftsmen working at St Paul's, it is not beyond the realms of possibility that if an Italian Garden was being constructed at Blenheim , some of the skilled craftsmen involved could be survivors of our wreck. This exquisite statue is of the Italian style and was probably carved by an Italian sculptor. Letters written by the Duke of Marlborough to his wife, also mentions of one block of marble to be made into a statue to be positioned inside the building.

I am curious to know if there is any white Carrara marble within Cors y Gedol. It is generally known that timbers from the wreck were used in building works there from 1711, and that pewter, silverware and a large table found their way into every day use at the Mansion. I am of the opinion that at least 80 tons of marble from the wreck was salvaged in the days after it grounded and all this was swiftly transported to London. Vaughan would know it belonged to the Crown and he did not want to be seen stealing any of it. After all, he was the Kings representative in that area.

I am convinced there are diaries of William Vaughan of Cors y Gedol to be seen somewhere. Although previously a High Sheriff, he was Keeper of Harlech Castle in 1709. All Harlech Castle documents and Cors y Gedol manuscripts require careful research.

Some conclusions, not yet verified.

Although owned by Genoa merchants the ship was built in Croatia. The compliment on board was at least 130. Soldiers and bombardiers on board may have been Italian.

During 1708 Sir Christopher Wren through his agents in Genoa ordered a consignment of white Carrara marble. Specific sizes to be used as floor tiles or building blocks for the altar platform at St Paul's were cut at the Tuscany quarries. These, together with a shipment of paper, left Leghorn in the first week of January 1709. To avoid unnecessary problems of capture by the French, the Bronze Bell ship took a route away from the French coastline and was destined for Dublin. There is evidence to support she had naval protection up to the southern end of St George's Channel. Meeting strong Westerly winds and overcast conditions for five days, a very slight under allowance for leeway caused the ship to be on the wrong side of the Irish Sea. First land sighted was Snowdonia. The captain tried unsuccessfully to extract the ship from being embayed inside Sarn Badrig. The weather had subsided and there were not strong winds or big surf, but there was a large swell. It is difficult to determine if this was before or after February 3rd, when a strong Westerly was blowing. While negotiating the inner channel near Bennar Beach the ship grounded on unforeseen underwater rocks. The ship could not be got off the underwater reef. A bower anchor was deliberately placed palm down and lashed amidships to prop up the hull and to keep the vessel upright. Local boats came out to help and took crew and soldiers ashore. Although the ship carried over 130 men, nobody was drowned.

As the vessel was upright, part of her cargo could be lifted out of the hold using the ship's masts with block and tackle. The captain knew this would help lighten the vessel and also save some of the valuable marble blocks. Vaughan, Lord of the Manor's residence at Cors y Gedol overlooked the beach and all arrangements for salvage had to go through him. Before the next bad weather hit the wreck a good proportion of the statue marble had been recovered.

When the vessel broke up and her hull disappeared beneath the waves, no more salvage of the cargo was carried out. A Welsh trading sloop sent news and some survivors to Dublin. Government agents in Dublin sent a ship to help with salvage of the cargo and masts. It was a relatively easy arrangement for the Bronze Bell Ship crew to get back to Genoa on ships leaving Dublin. There were at least ten ships a year going to Genoa or Leghorn, directly from Dublin. Within a month the salvaged marble was shipped from Dublin to London. It took about six days to sail from Dublin to London. The yard at Scotland Yard in the centre of London was where large items from wrecked ships and goods from recently captured prizes were temporarily stored. It was a secure yard surrounded by soldiers and King's men and nothing left there until all duty and proper Custom's documents had been stamped. In the Treasury Books dated 11th April 1709, Christopher Wren was asked to arrange sending eight marble blocks to Blenheim House and a further three long marble blocks to St Paul's to construct the Queen Anne Statue. It is not certain that these were the same blocks that had been salvaged out of the Bronze Bell wreck, but I think, quite likely. It is also possible that other blocks had already arrived in London, perhaps unloaded at Woolwich quay and had gone directly to St Paul's, their original destination.

Timbers over the next two years washed onto the beach and these were used in the construction of buildings at Cors y Gedol from 1711.

Bronze Bell Wreck   TOM BENNETT

When nearing the completion of this text, I sent a draft to Tony Iles for his comments. He alerted me to the fact that he considers the swivel guns, which he has studied in detail, do not belong to the Bronze Bell wreck. I think he may be correct, and they arrived on the wreck site at a date perhaps 200 years earlier than the Bronze Bell Wreck. The most important evidence to support this theory is the fact that all five guns recovered were loaded ready for action. All having wax at the touch holes and a lead apron cover over the breach, to keep the powder dry. Although we may think that an armed merchantman of 30 guns in 1700 is likely to have small swivel guns on her upper deck, this may not be the case. The swivel guns have been dated reasonably accurately to 1460 to 1490 era, so they would be about two hundred years old in 1675. Cautious gunners around 1709 are not going to risk firing such ancient armoury for fear of them blowing themselves up rather than an adversary. The only other reasons for them being on board the Bronze Bell ship are for ballast or as an antique collection for the Tower of London Armouries Department. In either case they would not be primed for action. The larger cannon had fallen on top of some of the swivel guns, indicating that the swivel guns were already there before the iron cannon. Tony Iles has suggested the dates of the swivel guns coincides with the dates that Jasper Tudor was landing near Harlech. Over a period of a decade Jasper Tudor could have visited more than once Bennar Beach. Its remoteness makes it an ideal secret landing place, especially if visiting Harlech Castle. The vessel could have been a French transport vessel with a set of six swivel guns. It would not be a huge deep draughted vessel that grounded but more likely a smaller vessel deliberately scuppered after landing or one that sank while anchored off the beach.

If we have two wrecks at the site then the Bronze Bell Designation, unwittingly, is protecting two historic wrecks. There could be another bronze bell to be found of the earlier wreck, a ship's bell which would be older than any other found in UK waters. This earlier wreck seems to have Royalty connections and brings another interesting dimension into the Maritime Heritage of this coastline.

This is a 15th Century French Cog. If the six swivel guns are from a previous wreck on the Bronze Bell site the vessel may have looked like this. Four swivel guns on the poop deck and two positioned on the fore-castle. The vessel may have been deliberately sunk off Bennar Beach in the summer of 1463 when Jasper Tudor landed near Harlech in one of three vessels sponsored by Louis XI. Jasper is thought to have

landed near Harlech Castle and then collected supporters to march on Denbigh Castle. Denbigh Castle stayed intact but with 2,000 strong he did burn down the town of Denbigh. After disembarkation of French soldiers landing near Harlech Castle, the vessel may have been sunk before daybreak so as not to alarm local inhabitants of a 'foreign' invasion. As he was to march inland there was no further need for the vessel. In 1461 King Edward IV came to the throne for the first time and Jasper fled to Ireland and spent the next few years living as a hunted fugitive. He reappeared in 1468, landing in North Wales to try and relieve Harlech Castle (the valiant defence of the garrison was the inspiration for the song 'Men of Harlech'). These are just some of the many occasions when Jasper was in the environs of Barmouth and Ty Gwyn. Armed Irish and French vessels were known to be near Harlech in the 15th Century with Jasper's capers. It is not beyond the realms of possibility that it was one of his ships that sank in the region. It is sheer coincidence, however that a Jasper vessel happened to land on the seabed in the same position as the Bronze Bell Ship some 226 years later. It is somewhat ironic that Ty Gwyn revels in the idea that Jasper hid there one night. It may be the permanent resting place of a swivel gun that he sat on whilst sailing to Barmouth in the 15th Century. Is another ship's bell from this vessel going to be found in the future?

Bronze Bell Wreck   TOM BENNETT

Bronze Bell Basics (the author's supposition)
Type: Three-masted Armed Merchantman
Port: Genoa.   Nationality: Republic of Genoa.
Ownership: Company of Genoa. Ship known as "A"
Ship on Charter to British Government:. No Name assigned.
Date of building: 1677
Place of building: Ragusa, Dubrovnik, Croatia
Size of vessel: 650 tons. (Ie. Smaller than 700 tons)
Dimensions: 108 feet long, by 31 feet beam. (33 m x 9.5 m)
Number of sails: 24. Number of guns: 24-30
Number of anchors: 6
Crew numbers: 80 sailors with 50 Militia, 130 total
Genoese crew, Italian military men.
From: Leghorn, Livorno, Italy. Destined: Dublin, Ireland.
Date of Departure: first week of January 1709.
Grounded at Talybont: 1st February 1709.
Broke up and sank Talybont: 20th February 1709.
Fatalities: If any loss of life, less than 8 drowned.
Cargo: Marble, paper, wines, soap, ladies hats, olive oil. All part salvaged.
Name of Captain: Not identified, but could have sailed Leghorn to Dublin and Leghorn to Amsterdam on previous voyages with the same ship.

When Vaughan's daily diaries are seen we may find a totally different scenario and more about what was salvaged.

If my theories are wildly incorrect then the ship broke up quickly on a different date in 1709, with a dreadful loss of life.

It has been an enjoyable journey piecing together some of the anomalies concerning the wreck site. My intention to find more about the date of sinking and the name of the ship has been accomplished. I have gained considerable understanding about trade with Leghorn and the likely location of where the ship was built and where the bell was cast.

I surmise that the date of grounding was between January 26th and 14th February 1709. There were strong Westerlies on the 3rd February 1709 and the ship ended up near a lee shore. However I do not think the ship stranded in gale force winds, and broke apart quickly.

If manuscripts relating to the Vaughans are researched properly, more will be revealed. I would be interested to see if some of my theories are borne out when more facts come to light. Further research may reveal two wrecks on the wreck site. Even if CADW persist in not allowing any excavation at the site there is ample scope for more local investigation and also analysis of marble thought to have gone to London. I am sure that the marble was intended for St Paul's in the first place and despite the ship being lost in Wales, it would be nice to confirm that some of her cargo still arrived in London .

As for the ship's name, in a lifetime of studying shipwrecks I have never before come across a ship that had no name! We cannot call our ship "No Name Ship" it has to be officially named. Now its name will remain Bronze Bell Wreck.

Written and compiled by Tom Bennett in 2017.

If you wish to make comments or contact the author, please do not hesitate to do so. Contact : Happyfish42@hotmail.com .
To contact Barmouth Sailors' Institute; enquires@barsailinst.org.uk

References

Baker, Thomas, Piracy and Diplomacy in 17th century North Africa.
Bennett, Tom., 2016 . Bells from pre 1830 Shipwrecks, Google e book.
Bennett,Tom., 2017 Maritime History of Newport Pembrokeshire.
Bennett Tom, 2015 Silver Dollars of Rhossili, Wales.   Amazon.
Griffith, J.E., Peds. Anglesey and Caern. Fams. 279; Arch. Camb. ser. 4, vi. 13–14, 16; ser. 1, ii. 132.
Hoffman, William J. " 'Palatine' Emigrants to America from the Principality of Nassau-Dillenburg,"
Holden, C., 2003, The Essential Underwater Guide to North Wales, Volume 1: Barmouth to South Stack, Calgo Publications.
Illsley, J.S., 1982, 'Admiral Lord Edward Russell and the building of St. Paul's Cathedral', Mariner's Mirror, 68.3: 305-315.
Konstam, A., 1988, Site Excavation Report of the Bronze Bell site, Gwynedd, unpublished Licensee report. Document within NA/GEN/2005/002e.
Konstam, A.,1989. Publisher Journal of the Ordnance ...A gunner's rule from the 'Bronze Bell' wreck, Tal-y-Bont, Gwynedd.
Larn, R. and Larn, B., 2000, Shipwreck Index of the British Isles, Volume 5 – West Coast and Wales, Lloyd's Register of Shipping.
London Gazette. All newspapers from 1st Jan to 1st April 1709.
Smith, R.D., 2004, 'The Wrought-Iron Swivel Guns from the Bronze Bell Wreck Site', Maritime Wales 25: 21-26.
http://aalims.org/uploads/Cihan%20Artunc%20Berat.pdf
Jobling HJW. The history and development of English anchors: ca 1550-1850. MA Thesis, Texas A&M University, 1993 pp 1-151.
http://www.narhvalen.dk/mystery-18th-century-shipwreck-found-gulf-finland-documentation-reveals-pristine-details.

Wignall, S. 1979, The Bronze Bell Wreck: Archaeological Survey of a late 17th century shipwreck lying in Cardigan bay, unpublished Licensee report. Document within NA/GEN/2005/002e.

Wessex Archaeology, 2006, Report on the Bronze Bell Wreck, Talybont North Wales. CADW.

Wessex Archaeology, 2004, 'Tal-y-Bont, Cardigan Bay, Designated Assessment: Preliminary Report', Unpublished Report ref 53111.02t.

Ragusan ships built for Oliver Cromwell's navy,, reference Roucek, in Kerner (ed.), Yugoslavia, p.136; Adamic, Native's Return, p. 152.

Fenwick, V. and Gale, A., 1999, Historic Shipwrecks: Discovered, Protected, and Investigated, Tempus Publishing, pg122-3

Mullen, R. 1993, Echoes of a Bronze Bell, Scuba World, July 1993 pg 28-30

Nichols, M., 1984, The Bronze Bell Wreck, Popular Archaeology, January 1984, pg34-6.

Mariners Mirror Vol 68 p 309.

The following manuscripts, formerly at Mostyn Hall , Flintshire but now in the National Library of Wales , were at
Cors y Gedol — Mostyn MSS. 115, 130, 131, 144 ('Llyfr Coch Nannau'), 145 ('Llyfr Gwyn Corsygedol'),
147, 160, 162, 163 ('Y Llyfr Gwyrdd'), 164 and 165 (this last an important volume from the family history standpoint). The literary tradition is continued in the 18th century in the person of William Vaughan (1707 -1775), who was Member of Parliament for Merioneth from 1734 to 1768.
Chirk Castle Accts. 1666–1753 ed. Myddelton, 455; Marlborough–Godolphin Corresp. 81, 88; Arch. Camb.ser. 4, vi. 14.
A Treatise of Ship's Anchors. George Cotsell   free download
https://www.thegazette.co.uk/London/issue/4651/page/2

For titles of books by TOM BENNETT go to website
www.shipwrecksforwalkers.co.uk